ADAPTING TO CHANGE

Making It Work For You

Carol Kinsey Goman, Ph.D.

ADAPTING TO CHANGE
Making It Work For You

Carol Kinsey Goman, Ph.D.

CREDITS
Editor: Beverly Manber
Layout and Composition: Recorder Typesetting
Cover Design: Barbara Ravizza
Artwork: Signe Wilkinson

Distribution to the U.S. Trade:

National Book Network, Inc.
4720 Boston Way
Lanham, MD 20706
1-800-462-6420

Library of Congress Catalog Card Number 92-054361
Goman, Carol Kinsey
ISBN 1-56052-192-9

This book is printed on recyclable paper with soy ink.

Dedication

I was a teenager when my father was fired from the **San Francisco Examiner**. The newspaper's entire circulation department had been eliminated, and my beloved parent was out of work. I will never forget the day. I came home from school to find my father already there. Not only was he home, he was in the kitchen. In fact, he was at the sink, bent over, with his head in his hands.

My heart went out to him, but as I was about to say something consoling, I noticed that the reason he was at the sink was that my sister was dying his grey hair brown so that he would look younger when he went looking for work. He straightened up, winked at me, and said: "Now we're going to have some fun."

And fun we had indeed, for my father did many fascinating things, including owning the "backyard" of a traveling circus, managing a gold mine, and taking photographs for postcards. At the age of 68, he opened his last business—a carnival supply company, which he operated successfully until his death—in the middle of a workday—at the age of 80.

My mother worked right alongside my father in most of his endeavors. After his death, she did what any grieving widow in her seventies would do—she took up country-western dancing. And a couple of years ago, she married her dance partner.

Having the profound luck of being raised by these two loving and incredibly resilient people is something for which I will always be grateful.

This book is dedicated to my wonderful "change-adept" parents, who made continuous change seem like a great adventure.

Acknowledgments

In 1987, I contacted a media cartoonist, whose work I had admired in the *San Jose Mercury*. By the time I found Signe Wilkinson, she had moved to Philadelphia and was an editorial cartoonist for the *Philadelphia Daily News*. Our collaboration on the book *Change-Busting: 50 Ways to Sabotage Organizational Change,* took place solely over the telephone. It was one of the easiest projects I have ever worked on. The illustrations that I have used in this book are reprinted from *Change-Busting*.

It was with real delight that I read that Signe Wilkinson had been awarded the 1992 Pulitzer Prize for editorial cartooning—it was the first time in history that a woman had won in this category. In honor of her talent, I salute Signe. In appreciation for her contribution to many of my works, I sincerely thank her.

CONTENTS

Introduction

This book is about accepting change.

The pace of change is accelerating. The lifespan of technology is shortening from its already brief eighteen-month term. Global competition has only just begun to affect the way we do business. American companies will continue to restructure. The demographic makeup of the workforce bears little resemblance to that of twenty years ago. The relationship between employees and their organizations is changing from one based on a long-term agreement to one that acknowledges the temporary nature of most business liaisons.

The above are facts. The first step to making change work for you is to face facts—to learn to accept the world the way it is—and then to look for ways to make reality serve you.

This book is designed to help you not only survive, but to thrive on ongoing change.

My approach to personal change-management is based on fifteen years of studying and working with thousands of people in private counseling sessions, and in programs I have conducted for corporations and professional associations around the world.

In my private practice, I have worked with individuals facing transitions in their personal and professional lives. These people have gone through major changes in their careers, health, financial status, relationships or spiritual condition.

Until the mid-1980s, my work had been with people struggling to cope with change. In 1985, I began to focus on organizational change—mergers, restructurings, downsizings, shifts in product lines, strategy and process—and especially on those employees who were *change-adept* within the organization—resilient, healthy and productive, even under vast amounts of workplace change. I interviewed hundreds of change-adept professionals, and compiled a profile of their work strategies and attitudes. In the process, I developed a series of speeches and seminars, under the titles: "Surviving and Thriving on Change," "Workforce 2000: Changing Values, Roles, and Responsibilities," and "Managing Continuous Change."

To date, these programs have been presented in 128 different organizations: Fortune 500 companies, hospitals, universities, national and international professional associations, and government agencies. I have given speeches and seminars in seven countries, and have addressed audiences of chief executive officers, as well as audiences consisting solely of secretaries.

This book grows out of that work. It represents my research findings—factors common to those who handle change best—and techniques I have used successfully to help people develop their own change-adeptness.

Carol Kinsey Goman, Ph.D.

Chapter 1 < A CLIMATE OF CHANGE

"We're in one of those great historical periods that occur every 200 to 300 years when people don't understand the world anymore, when the past is not sufficient to explain the future."
—Peter Drucker, Claremont Graduate Center Professor

"It's not so much that we're afraid of change or so in love with the old ways, but it's that place in between that we fear. . . It's like being between trapezes. It's Linus when his blanket is in the dryer. There's nothing to hold on to."
—Marilyn Ferguson, Author and futurist

IN THE PAST DECADE:

- Nearly 50 percent of all U.S. companies were restructured
- Over 80,000 firms were acquired or merged
- At least 700,000 organizations sought bankruptcy protection to continue operating
- Over 450,000 organizations failed
- More than 24 million jobs were lost

IN THE NEXT DECADE:

- At least one-fourth of all current "knowledge" and accepted "practice" will be obsolete
- The life span of new technology will decrease from the current eighteen months
- Women will own over 50 percent of all businesses in the U.S.
- Entire industries will disappear and be replaced by others we have not heard of yet
- Twenty times as many people will be working at home
- A majority of the entrants to the workforce will be women and minorities
- Dual-career couples will increase to 63 percent of all families
- The growth and development of a one-world economy will further increase global competition
- Organizational structures will undergo further transition

Living with Nonstop Change

"Change is the only constant." The Greek philosopher Heraclitus made this comment 2,500 years ago. It could not be more true today. Change is the most pervasive influence within today's workplace. Profound changes are shaking up our lives and the way we do business. And the pace of change is picking up. Accelerated change will continue to be driven by sharp economic swings, new competitive pressures, new technologies, government regulations, sociocultural shifts, further globalization of the marketplace, and the continued reshaping of businesses worldwide.

Business expert Peter Drucker says, "We are entering a 'post capitalist' era in which organizations will have to innovate quickly and be global." And while companies continue to merge, downsize and restructure to meet the challenges of globalized competition, the workforce must constantly adjust to the unpredictable. Employees can no longer expect lifetime or even long-term employment. Nor can they expect stability. Change has become a fact of corporate life, to be accepted and dealt with.

In the 1980s, when I first addressed organizations about workplace change, there was a lot of interest in the topic. Both managers and employees were looking for ways to help cope with upcoming change, so that, as soon as possible, everyone could get through the change and return to business as usual. Today, that scenario is different. When I address national conferences or speak to organizations here and abroad, I know that people are looking for ways to help everyone understand that change *is* business as usual. Large and small changes overlap one another until it is all change, from margin to margin.

So, whether we like it or not, and regardless of whether or not we handle it well, we work in an environment of continuous, accelerating change.

Take a moment and test yourself. How many of the following changes can you already see in your workplace?

From:	To:
Lively, local competition	Fierce, global competition
Slow change	Accelerated pace of change
Giving/Following orders	Empowerment/Responsibility
Few choices	Multiple choices and options
Product-driven decisions	Consumer-driven decisions
Hierarchical structure	Self-managed work teams
Rugged individual	Team player
Rigid rules	Flexible rules as guidelines
Revere the status quo	Continuous improvement
Moderate skill level	Higher skill level needed
Moderate work load	"Do more with less"
Mass marketing	Niches, specialty markets
Narrow specialization	A total systems view
Paternalistic management	Partnership, shared values
Creative thinking from top management only	Creative thinking required of all employees
Sequential changes	Overlapping changes

Change-Adept Professionals

People react very differently to change. Many people feel a frightening loss of control and resistance to the actual or perceived threat inherent in change. They struggle unsuccessfully to maintain the status quo. They cling to obsolete rules and structure, rather than confront an ambiguous environment. They search for absolute predictability in a time of constant chaos. Frustrated and pressured, they burn out. They are victims of change . . . and they do not know why.

By contrast, some people take control of change with appropriate attitudes, work styles and health practices. They build greater resilience. Not only do they survive, but they actually thrive in changing times. While their co-workers are overwhelmed by the negative aspects of change, the *change-adept* capitalize on opportunities they encounter daily.

It is no mere accident, no random selection by fate as to whom will adapt optimally. Rather, there are specific *characteristics and strategies*, common to change-adept people, which account *for their personal and professional success*. These traits and skills can be developed in anyone.

For the past fifteen years, I have worked with individuals and organizations going through transitions. In charting the habits and attitudes of change-adept employees, I have developed their collective profile and shared my findings with audiences around the world. Globally, the issue of how to handle change well is seen as crucial to the success of the individual employee, as well as to the entire organization.

Five factors characterize the change-adept employee. While these may come naturally to some, those who have developed them through conscious training efforts handle change just as well. The next five chapters of this book focus on the *five factors of change-adeptness*, and offer techniques to amplify your current ability in each particular area. The five factors are:

Confidence
Challenge
Coping
Counterbalance
Creativity

THE PROCESS OF CHANGE

Change requires an individual to go through the emotional process of transition. This process is normal and natural, with predictable stages of grieving. The more you understand this process, and anticipate its progress, the more prepared you will be to facilitate the emotional stages. Chapter 7 defines these stages of transition and suggests strategies for minimizing the distress.

Chapter 8 examines changing employee values and lifestyle factors that cause many people to redefine success and to make different business-related choices. It focuses on proactive ways to take control of change, explaining the steps necessary for successful change and the emotional process of positive transitions.

TENETS OF CHANGE

Every author has a set of perceptions and prejudices about the topic he or she is addressing. Following is a summary of my underlying beliefs about workplace change, so you will understand the predisposition of this book:

- Change is no longer a force in the business environment. It *is* the business environment.
- Change is global. Organizations everywhere—in various industries, at all corporate levels and in every industrialized nation—are going through change.
- *The most difficult behaviors to change are those responsible for past success.*
- The pace of change is accelerating. If you stand still, you will soon be obsolete.
- *The best time to change is before you have to.*
- Your reaction to change is totally within your control.
- *You do not have to like change to deal with it successfully;* however, you must accept it.
- Almost no one likes change done *to* him or her. Almost everyone likes change done *by* them.
- If change is inevitable and you strive for stability, you set yourself up for change to come in the form of a crisis.
- *The only real security in changing times is that which you develop within yourself.*

A CHECKLIST

☐ Have I accepted the fact that nonstop change is the unavoidable reality today?

☐ Do I honestly think of the status quo as only a temporary resting place in a time of constant change?

☐ Do I understand that the continual updating of skills is a requirement of today's workplace?

☐ Do I have enough information about global competition and how it is affecting my industry and profession?

☐ Am I ready to explore new ways of seeing my life and my options?

Chapter 2 < CONFIDENCE

"The trick to handling change is confidence. You must assess your strengths and focus on what you do best."
—Executive, Bank of America

"I have confidence in my abilities and I know my market value."
—Manager, Information Line

What personality trait is most responsible for your ability to deal well with change? In my interviews with change-adept people, the answer I heard most often was *confidence*. It was also the easiest to spot. Confident people are self-motivated and willing to take risks. Quite simply, they know how good they are.

In the workplace, self-confident employees are often those who feel secure in the "portability" of their skills, whose professional networks are intact, and who know they will survive professionally, even if it means finding a new position. They recognize their value to the organization, and have a realistic perception of their worth in the marketplace. Because they focus on their strengths and develop their talents, they have an obvious advantage over those of us who fixate on our limitations and are paralyzed by mistakes.

If You Believe You Can Or Cannot, You Are Right

Research at the UCLA Brain Research Institute indicates that the creative capacity of the human brain is potentially limitless—*the only restrictions are self-imposed through our belief systems*. The biggest obstacle you may ever have to face is your absolute acceptance of what you believe to be your limits.

People behave in accordance with their perception of reality, rather than with reality itself. A Manitoba Canadian Longitudinal Study of Aging found that a patient's belief that he or she was healthy was a greater predictor of future health than anything else—including doctors' examinations and laboratory reports.

One of my clients was a real estate salesman who believed he would not be able to understand how to operate the new computer system in his company. "I've never done well in any classroom situation. I'm just too dumb to learn." This man was a highly successful salesperson and not "dumb" at all. He had an older sister who had been the "star pupil" of the family. Because his grades never compared to those of his sibling, his parents repeatedly told him that he was "the athletic one" and his sister "the smart one." After a while, he believed it.

Self-image may bear little resemblance to what you are, but *it will always be a precise reflection of how you evaluate yourself*. In any given area, this evaluation is prone to inaccuracy, since you began gathering data at a very early age. In your childhood, the information you accepted as true was assimilated literally. Positively or negatively, the labels acquired in childhood are often incorporated into an evolving self-image and acted out for a lifetime. Many people who were told that they "were not good at sports" took this so literally that for years they refused to participate in any sport. A few were amazed to find, much later in life, that failing at grammar school volleyball had absolutely nothing to do with their current aptitude for skiing or golf.

Your belief system is formulated through a mixture of childhood impressions, recurrent input by family, peers and authority figures. This input is subject to both accurate and inaccurate self-evaluation. *These beliefs create your self-image. Your self-image includes a lack or an abundance of confidence.*

Confidence-building begins with an analysis of currently held beliefs about your abilities and talents. As you answer the following questions, keep in mind that one way to change a poor self-image is to *acknowledge* the influence of past input and recognize its subjective nature. Ask yourself: Are the family members, etc. who most influenced you infallible? Could they have been wrong? Could they have been accurate, but in one context only and at one point in time? How might you have embellished or misunderstood what was happening?

♦ What was your childhood nickname? (If you did not have one, what nickname would have been appropriate?) Mortimer schnerd
♦ What was your label? ("The ___Shy___ one.")
♦ What beliefs do you hold about yourself that destroy or reduce your confidence? How might you check the accuracy of those beliefs?
♦ What beliefs do you hold about yourself that build or enhance confidence? If you focus on these productive beliefs *more* than the limiting beliefs, you can start to change your self-image in the direction of increased confidence.
♦ What beliefs would you like to hold about yourself? If you could, how would you change your self-image? By entertaining the possibility of these changes, and by thinking of yourself as growing in that direction, you change your self-image in the direction of increased confidence.

Competence and Confidence

I gave a speech for the top management team of a company in Northern California. A few days later the president of the company telephoned me to say, "As you know, the company's been acquired by an organization that is relocating us to another state. After your presentation last week, I began thinking. I have an administrative assistant who is probably the brightest, most creative person I have worked with. The problem is, she's married and doesn't want to move her family out of the Bay Area. I was wondering if you would see her for a private session, so that when she applies for a new job, she will come across just as terrific as she really is. I will pay for the session."

Of course, I agreed, and looked forward to meeting this talented woman. When she came into the office, I said, "This is a real pleasure. I've heard so many nice things about you. Tell me about yourself. What is it you do best that you'd want a new prospective employer to know?" This very bright, highly creative woman did not answer immediately. She was silent for several seconds before saying, "I don't know. I do a lot of things well, but when I do them, I don't notice."

Competence has little to do with confidence. The fact that you do your job very well does not, by itself, guarantee that you are also confident of your abilities. It is only when people are aware of their competence that they are confident.

What do you remember most clearly—your greatest achievement or your most humiliating defeat? While most of us can recite a litany of our failings and shortcomings, confident people are more aware of their strengths and successes. They notice the things they do well. They recognize and reward their own achievements.

Lee Strasberg, the famous acting coach said, "I can train anything except that for which you have no talent." All of us have areas of lesser and greater talents. It can be helpful to acknowledge our weaknesses, and seek guidance or training to develop those areas. However, there is nothing more frustrating than to strive to excel in areas for which you have little or no talent.

There are at least four different ways to deal with weaknesses: 1) Choose an assignment that will demand you correct your shortcomings; 2) hire or develop people who balance out your weaknesses; 3) consider a class, workshop or book addressed to building those skills; and 4) choose assignments in which weaknesses do not matter.

Management guru Peter Drucker advocates the fourth way: "Don't focus on building up your weaknesses," he writes. "Understand your strengths and place yourself in a position where those strengths count. Your strengths will carry you through to success."

You can elevate self-confidence by becoming more aware of your current accomplishments and talents. Here is a simple personal inventory:

♦ Review your accomplishments during the past year. Make a list of your successes.
♦ What are your greatest strengths and qualities?
♦ What do others say are your greatest strengths? Ask co-workers and friends outside of work; do they see the same things?
♦ What talents do you use most in your current job?
♦ What talents do you use infrequently or not at all?
♦ How could you use your talents more?
♦ Where might your strengths be most useful?
♦ How do you reward your successes?
♦ When going through past changes, what internal and external resources helped you the most?

What You See is What You Get

Visualization is the technique in which you make full sensory mental images. While imagery skills have long been an integral part of many motivational programs, brain researchers have only recently verified that pictures held in the mind contribute uniquely to an individual's confidence and success.

Edmund Jacobson, an American physiologist, found that people who vividly imagine themselves running, replicating mentally the five physical senses and incorporating the emotional experience of the event, undergo subtle but measurable muscular contractions, as if they were actually running. Biofeedback research with the Swiss Olympic ski team showed the brainwave patterns for skiers who were physically on a course to be identical with those of the same athletes who only graphically envisioned the ski run.

Vivid imagery is so sensory rich that it duplicates reality, with all the visual, auditory, tactile and emotional sensations congruent with the actual situation. Proficient imagers may even create odors and tastes associated with an event.

Visualization floods your brain and central nervous system with a sensory-accurate vision of what you desire to achieve. The brain then incorporates this image, as if it were already accomplished.

Stanford University neurophysiologist Karl Pribram believes that mental images precede and affect all actions. He refers to this phenomenon as *feed-forward*.

A classic experiment conducted with members of a high school basketball team had the players divided into three groups. One third of the team was instructed to practice free-throws for one hour every day. The second third imaged perfect free-throws daily, but were not allowed to handle the ball physically. The third group was told not to practice in any manner. At the end of a month, when all teams played again, the results were compared. The first two groups had improved equally, while the last third did not improve at all.

The brain and nervous system cannot distinguish between physical practice and vivid mental simulation, because they both fire the same neural connections in the autonomic nervous system.

Using imagery simulation to boost your self-confidence for an upcoming event is a simple procedure: *first, state your performance objective. Next, break your goal into its sensory components.* Then, relax and create a clear mental image, rich with distinct sensory data.

An executive for a software company was preparing to present an important proposal to a prospective client. Her performance goal was to present her proposal with authority and impact. The sensory components were:

♦ **Visual** - Seeing the interested faces of the client's management team and watching them nod in agreement

- ◆ **Auditory** - Hearing the sound of her own strong, steady voice
- ◆ **Kinesthetic** - Touching the smooth paper of her well-memorized notes
- ◆ **Olfactory** - Smelling the leather chairs in the conference room
- ◆ **Gustatory** - Tasting the flavor of her cup of coffee
- ◆ **Emotional** - Feeling steady, well-prepared, successful and totally focused

Visualization may not be everyone's chosen technique, but many business people use it as a natural part of preparation for any important meeting or interaction. If you would like to develop your skill in imagery, follow these steps:

STEP 1: State your performance objective. (My goal is _to get another job_

As tempting as it may be to state your objective in terms of other people's reaction, the only aspect you can control is your own part in the proceedings.
Do not say: My goal is to have my boss give me a raise.
Do say: My goal is to ask for a raise in an organized, convincing manner.

STEP 2: Break this objective into its sensory components.

Visual - I see _____.

Auditory - I hear _____.

Kinesthetic - I feel (touch) _____.

Olfactory - I smell _____.

Gustatory - I taste _____.

Emotional - I feel _____.

Several styles of sensory perception are often referred to as *representational systems*. They correspond with the sensory categories in this technique. People tend to perceive reality most strongly through one of these forms.

When you are developing your sensory components, some will come easier to you than others. If you are basically visual, it will be easier for you to create an image. If you are predominantly auditory, the sounds or words used in a situation will be the easiest to recall or to construct. Kinesthetic people remember the way something felt, either tactile sensations or emotions—internal sensations—and find it most natural to utilize that information. The two minor representational systems, olfactory and gustatory, are seldom one's primary form. Start with whichever form is easiest, and add the others as they occur to you.

Of course, you can improve your recall and imagery in all sensory modes. You can practice by mentally recalling primary colors, the house of your childhood, the face of your best friend; the tune of your favorite song, the sound of your mother's voice, the crash of waves; the feel of ice cubes, sandpaper, a kitten's fur; the fragrance of your favorite perfume or aftershave lotion, freshly baked bread, a lemon; the flavor of your favorite ice cream, tooth-paste, coffee; the predominant emotion on your first day at a new job, your happiest holiday, falling in love.

STEP 3. Create a focused mental image, incorporating full sensory input.

Research has found two factors that are especially important for effective imagery simulation: relaxation and repetition.

Relaxation - You need to relax deeply enough to bypass the critical function of the conscious mind and directly access the subconscious. This is neither esoteric nor difficult. Simply find a comfortable place to sit or lie down, close your eyes and take a few deep breaths. As you exhale, begin to purposefully release tension from your head, your arms, the trunk of your body and finally your legs. Focus on the pleasant sensations associated with relaxing and letting go of tension. Now imagine you are entering a motion picture theater to preview your upcoming event. First, create your scene visually, then step into the picture and mentally experience all the other sensory components of your successful performance.

Repetition - As a small child, you learned to dress yourself. Buttoning buttons, tying shoe-laces and zipping zippers took conscious effort. After some period of time, you had dressed yourself correctly so often that this behavior pattern registered in the subconscious level of your mind as a habit, no longer requiring conscious attention.

Repeating the imagery process on a daily basis is the mental dress rehearsal component of your overall preparation. Repetition helps to subconsciously implant the vision of accomplishment, so that you more quickly develop the *habit* of self-confidence.

On the Mark, Get Set, Fail

You may choose to focus your attention selectively on those beliefs which elevate self-esteem. You may increase your awareness of your talents. You may even repeatedly visualize your confident behaviors. Still, you will undoubtedly experience failures, setbacks and slumps. How you deal with these failures and disappointments—how you prepare for them, evaluate them, review them later and file them in your memory bank—is crucial to your self-confidence.

In my research, I found that change-adept people not only *expect failure;* many of them actively encourage it. Referred to by Tom Peters as the *ready, fire, aim* method, this approach puts an idea into immediate action, to learn quickly how far off the mark it is. Mary Kay Ash, founder of Mary Kay Cosmetics, is one who considers failure a valuable lesson. She has a *fail forward* philosophy that allows errors, mistakes and setbacks to serve as guides for improved future actions. While no one likes failure, everyone fails repeatedly. The trick is to acknowledge your errors, learn from them, and release them as soon as possible.

How well you handle failures and setbacks depends a lot on how well you have prepared for them. Several years ago, as a program presenter for a conference in Dallas, I was in the audience of the man speaking before me. Although I have long forgotten the name of this speaker, I remember clearly the closing of his program: "I have been speaking to you today about power. We've discussed the various kinds of power you might have within your organizations. But there is one last kind of power we haven't talked about. And in many ways, it is the most important of all. If you don't have this kind of power, you will never have any other kind. It is 'exit power.' If you don't know exactly what you would do if you were fired, then you will always be at the mercy of the organization and will never have any real power within it."

Exit power showed up again in my interviews with people who survived and thrived on change. In this time of business mergers, acquisitions and restructurings, it is crucial to anticipate and prepare for the possibility of being outplaced. Indeed, I found that those who were the most confident and productive under the threat of organizational upheaval had a realistic view of their value to the company, knew their worth in the marketplace, had resumes that were up-to-date, nurtured business and personal networks, and had enough money in the bank to survive until they found new jobs.

Risky Business

In times of change and uncertainty, it is increasingly *important to take professional risks.* Innovative ideas, higher levels of personal performance, and increased professional visibility can all bring substantial rewards. They all also involve risk.

Confident people take risks more readily than do their less confident colleagues. This is especially apparent when organizations are going through reorganization. Employees live within a changing environment, uncertain about their futures with the newly structured company. More confident employees tend to speak up, to question and to offer suggestions; less confident people tend to keep a "low profile," trying to be as inconspicuous as possible.

Most people avoid taking risks because of two predominant factors: the effort and discomfort required to leave their *"comfort zones," and fear of the consequences of failure. These factors are present, to some degree, for everyone.*

We all tend to gravitate toward our comfort zones. Most people like dining in restaurants where they are known. They feel most at ease in familiar surroundings. They tend to enjoy people who are like them, who share similar viewpoints and ideas. When vacationing abroad, many travelers stay in hotels that most resemble their hometown accommodations.

Everyone battles with fear. It is universally the most powerful negative motivator. When *fear* becomes overwhelming, it distorts reality, inhibits action and erodes self-esteem. *Paralyzed, people totally stop taking risks—procrastinating even the smallest action steps.*

Fear is normal. It is an appropriate response whenever you do something new or risky. Expect it. There is nothing wrong with being afraid; it is how you react to fear that makes the difference. You can let your imagination run wild by magnifying the horrible dimensions and consequences. You can exaggerate the difficulty. You can dwell on your limitations. Or you can develop strategies for handling fear creatively.

A client named Vicky was being groomed by her father to take control of the family business. "This is a wonderful opportunity for me, but I'm so afraid that I'll let my father down. Sometimes I think that it would be easier for everyone if I just stayed in the background for a few more years. I know that I look confident and successful to other people, but inside I'm shaking like Jell-O."

The pressure Vicky was putting on herself was apparent. Although she had proven herself a competent businesswoman in a previous career, she was moving out of her comfort zone—her familiar area of expertise and ability—to another arena—in which she feared that her job performance could damage her relationship with her father.

After meeting with Vicky a few times, we developed a strategy to help her determine whether to take this risk. First, she wrote a "worry list," itemizing all the things that might go wrong. Beside each worry, Vicky wrote a response—if this happened, what would I do? How would I handle it?—Then, she had to decide whether or not she could survive the worst possible consequence of failure—that of performing beneath her father's expectations. While the negative consequences of failure are never enjoyable, they are seldom the life-threatening results we fantasize.

In Vicky's case I asked a few simple questions: "What would you do if you tried your best and still disappointed your father?" Vicky replied, "Why, I'd feel perfectly awful." I agreed that she would. Then I asked, "What would you do after you felt awful?" Vicky verbally wound through an entire process of reactions. She talked about leaving the country, changing her name, and finally joked about putting herself "up for adoption." "Good plan," I concurred. "Would you survive?"

Taking a deep breath, Vicky smiled and looked me straight in the eyes. "Yes. I guess I would."

Sometimes fears can be reduced by challenging their validity. Last year, in New Zealand, I watched as tourists went bungee-jumping. In this sport, one's ankles are tied together, then a bungee cord—a long "rubber band"—is attached to the bound ankles, and one jumps off of a high platform. It looked frightening and dangerous. "People could get killed," I thought. "At the very least, they must get whiplash when the bungee cord pulls them back up." This was not something that I would ever care to do.

After twenty minutes of observing the jumpers, I began to interview some of them. Did you hurt your back? *No.* Did you jerk your neck? *No. I'm telling you it's surprisingly gentle.* Has anyone ever been hurt at this location? *Never. The operators here are very professional.*

Was it difficult to make the jump? *Not once I was mentally committed to it.* Was it fun? *It's more than fun. It's the realization that I can rely on something inside me to take me beyond what I previously thought were my limits. Talk about expanding your comfort zone!*

Before a full thirty minutes had passed, I too was jumping off a bridge 132 feet above a raging river with my ankles hooked to a bungee cord. The experience was everything I had been told it was.

Not every risk is worth taking. The concept of *calculated risk* looks at the potential benefits, definite costs and probabilities of success which can be quantified. If the likelihood of failure is very high, the risk may be too great. Failure that is 90 percent probable should be considered differently from that which is only marginally possible. If the punishment for failing far exceeds the rewards for succeeding, the risk may not be worth our effort. Many people build commitment to taking a risk by making sure that the *payoff* is vitally important to them. If there is little reward, there may be little motivation. Sometimes, no action is taken because there is too much risk for too little reward. After this type of calculation, choosing not to risk is always a viable option.

If you decide to take the risk, make sure you do so with confidence. Understand that the discomfort you feel is the natural byproduct of your self-image stretching beyond its old comfort zone. Expect the fear to stay. Go into action in spite of your fears. Make friends with fear and take it with you. Make fun of it. Remind yourself that you can survive the worst possible consequences of failure. Just do it.

A letter was sent to me after I gave a speech in California. The author wrote: "I enjoyed and identified with your description of the need for a successful change-master to be a risk taker. I view risk as a means of self-growth and self-empowerment. A quote that has stuck with me for many years—and one I think of when faced with risk—is 'Taste death, Live life.' While it may sound moribund initially, death can mean something other than the cessation of life. I also think of the death one feels when embarrassed, when humiliated, or when one's ideas or endeavors fail. If you don't risk the potential of all these deaths, you'll never feel the magnificence of life."

My favorite risk-taking aid is the creation of a confidence trigger. To develop your *confidence trigger,* you first construct a full sensory image, from memory or fantasy, of precisely how you want to approach the risk. Think of a time when you took a risk and were incredibly successful, or pattern your image on another person who impresses you with his or her risk-taking assuredness.

Take a few minutes to fully absorb this *model of risk-taking success,* creating it in finite detail. Then, think the word *confidence* and attach it to this powerful image. Stay calm and feel confident and totally in control.

When you want to activate the confidence trigger, take a deep breath, slowly, through your nose. Hold the breath, expanding your lungs and straightening your posture. Exhale slowly through your mouth. As you do, keep your body erect, but release any excess tension. Let yourself relax. Then, think the word *confidence* and recall your risk-taking image. (I cannot tell you how many times I have fortified myself before taking a risk by thinking, "I can do this. I can do anything. I'm a bungee-jumper.")

Life = Experience

I am now going to pass along the best advice I ever received: A wise, elderly man advised me, long ago, to experience everything I could. "You know," he said, "I have never truly regretted one thing that I did. But I have a lot of regrets over things that I never tried."

I concur with my mentor. Experience everything you can. Do not limit yourself arbitrarily. You do not know, right now, what you will be doing in five or ten years, or what skills you will need to be successful. Experiences are not only life, they are lessons in living.

Are you taking intellectual risks? Do you read books, take courses and engage in stimulating conversations? Have you expanded your horizons by developing an appreciation and skills in art, theatre, gourmet cooking or computers?

Are you taking physical risks? Do you camp out, climb rocks, water-ski or take aerobics? Have you ever trained for and entered a race? Do you stretch yourself physically?

Are you taking emotional risks? Do you move out of your comfort zone by going to new places, meeting new people, starting conversations, expressing your ideas or disagreeing? Are you ever the first to say, "I love you"?

A CHECKLIST

☐ Can I list my greatest achievements?

☐ Am I aware of my talents?

☐ Do I have a realistic opinion of my value to this organization and to the market-place in general?

☐ Do I prepare for failures and setbacks?

☐ Am I a risk-taker?

☐ Do I have a strategy for dealing with fear?

Chapter 3   CHALLENGE

"This is the most exciting time ever."
    —Regional Vice President, A.T.&T

*"I never see change as a negative.
It is always an adventure."*
    —Entrepreneur

In Chinese, the ideogram for crisis combines two characters: One is the symbol for danger, the other for opportunity. The same dual aspects can be ascribed to change. With any change, the danger of possible reversals and losses coexists with incredible opportunities for personal and professional achievements.

When change-adept people are asked for words they associate *with change, they acknowledge the stress, uncertainty, pressure and disruption, and they emphasize the benefits—the opportunity, adventure, growth, excitement and challenge of change.*

Why do some people naturally view change as a challenge, while others see only the dangerous aspects? Much has to do with an overall attitude. *Are you an optimist or a pessimist?* If you have a positive mental attitude, you generally focus on the positive elements in any situation.

W. Clement Stone, president of Combined Insurance and author of numerous books, said, "There is very little difference in people. But that little difference makes a big difference. The little difference is attitude. The big difference is whether it is positive or negative."

It has been reported that former President Ronald Reagan's favorite joke was about two children—one a pessimist, the other an optimist. The first child was put in a room filled with toys. He complained that the toys were not good enough, that they would probably break or be stolen, and that he was bored and miserable. The second child was led to a room filled with horse manure. True to his character, he grabbed a shovel and exclaimed happily, "There's got to be a pony here somewhere!"

Obviously, you cannot control everything that happens to you. But you are in complete control of how you respond to what happens. You can choose to concentrate on the *dangers*—all those things that are going wrong, or, have the potential to do so. Or you can decide to look for the silver lining, and search out challenges and opportunities.

Suzanne Kobasa and Salvatore Maddi, authors of *The Hardy Executive: Health Under Stress*, studied groups of business executives in high stress jobs, who nonetheless remained robust and healthy. One stress-resistant resource that all of these hardy individuals shared was *the perception that perceived change was an unavoidable challenge to master, rather than a threat.*

Plus and Minus

One simple technique shared by many change-adept professionals that I interviewed was the *change balance sheet*. Try this for yourself: Take a sheet of paper and fold it lengthwise, down the middle. On one side of the page write the heading *Opportunities* and on the other side write *Dangers*. Think of a change going on at work, and list as many of its positive and negative components as you can. See if you can list several items for each category.

Look at your list of negatives. Make sure it is complete. Study the list and realize that it is understandable to be concerned about the potential dangers in a change. You might even find it helpful to formulate a contingency plan in case the dangers become actual. But can you see that there is usually no further benefit to you personally or professionally in continuing to dwell on negativity? As a matter of fact, the reverse is true. Coming to work every day with a bad attitude is mentally and physically exhausting. It poisons your job satisfaction, clouds your judgement and inhibits your creativity.

Look at your list of opportunities. See if you can add to that list by carrying it with you for a few days and giving it further consideration. Keep asking the question, "What other opportunities are there that I don't see yet?" Think of the positive aspects of this change for the company, for the customer, for your career, for you.

Truth in Labeling

As an avid baseball fan, one of my favorite stories concerns an interview with three umpires. The same question was put to all of them: "How do you decide which pitches are balls and which are strikes?" The first umpire thought for a while. "There are balls and there are strikes, and I calls 'em as I sees 'em." The second umpire disagreed. "There are balls and there are strikes, and I calls 'em as they is." The third umpire shook his head. "There are balls and there are strikes, but they ain't nothing until I calls 'em!"

Likewise with change, the way you mentally label a situation determines how you react. And the various ways people label the same set of circumstances will produce a variety of results—from distressful and destructive to healthful and life-enhancing.

One of my clients retired from an executive position; to him, it was the "end of my productive years." He proceeded through this traumatic adjustment, filled with uncertainty, self-doubt and, finally, physical ailments. His physician referred him to me for stress-reduction training.

Another client retired at approximately the same time. He viewed his retirement as a "golden opportunity" to travel, to consult, and—something he had been wanting to do for years—to learn a foreign language. His appointments with me were arranged by his golf pro to improve his game by learning mental rehearsal techniques.

Each person interprets events based on available information, as it is filtered by his or her viewpoint. It is human nature to subjectively filter data, *and believe that this "selective awareness" represents reality.* Of course it does not; it only reflects our individual perspective at the time.

Perspective can be altered with new experience. The vice president of a national insurance company told me he had been fired from a previous job in another industry. "I was afraid of being fired. To me, it was the worst thing that could ever happen. But when it actually occurred a couple of years ago, I found out I could put something together for myself that was better than I had before. *Believe me, change will never again be the enemy.*"

Do not be too quick to label a change negatively. Right now, it many seem that you are in the eye of a cyclone. You may feel the organization is "out to get you." You might look toward the future and feel disoriented and confused. But you cannot tell, in the middle of a change, how you will be affected when it is over. Looking back, you might even label this change as the most positive thing that ever happened to you. Who knows?

Even the most negative transition can afford a tremendous opportunity to redirect the course of your life. The general manager of an outplacement firm tells clients: "Before you jump into a job search for an exact replacement of what you left, ask yourself if that is what you really want to do. You may have had a job that was more comfortable than satisfying, more routine than challenging. What other talents do you have? What dreams have gone unaddressed? What do you really want to accomplish? What would be the most fun?"

As author and radio personality Garrison Keillor says, "Some luck lies in not getting what you thought you wanted, but getting what you have, which once you have got it you may be smart enough to see is what you would have wanted had you known."

What, Me Worry?

Those who handle change best *have constructed strategies for analyzing a situation, choosing a course of action and moving forward.* They do not dwell in "what might have been," nor do they divert valuable energy to negative possibilities.

At the other end of the spectrum, however, are those who cannot let go of a problem situation. They let worry build the circumstances out of proportion. They become hostile and highly critical of themselves and others. Just the threat of change can arouse anxiety in those who deplore ambiguity and uncertainty.

Worry can be bad for your health. The connection between mind and illness or wellness has been noted by physicians as early as Sir William Osler of nineteenth century England. He bluntly stated that "the cure of tuberculosis depends more on what the patient has in his head than what he has in his chest." In addition, modern scientists in a new field known as psychoimmunology are collecting intriguing evidence that the mind directly influences the body's disease-fighting immune system.

Take a few minutes and reflect on your current preoccupations and concerns. To the extent that these worries are occupying your thoughts and making claims on your energy, they detract from your optimal productivity and health.

Accentuate the Positive

Martin Seligman, a psychologist at the University of Pennsylvania, argues that management's best predictor of success is the employee's level of optimism. He developed an examination to identify upbeat people and sold it to Metropolitan Life to use in a pilot program. If these novice salespeople performed, the insurance carrier would agree to expand the program. Met Life used the 20-minute exam with 15,000 recruits—many of whom had failed the standard industry exam the first time around. Within months, the recruits were dramatically outselling those hired the traditional way.

Seligman's research shows the *power of self-fulfilling prophecies.* Those who believe they are masters of their fate are more likely to be successful than those who attribute results to forces beyond their control. Optimists see themselves in control of events, or at least not at the mercy of circumstances. Pessimists feel victimized by events and powerless to do anything about them.

Positive Imagery

Several years ago, Dr. O. Carl Simenton, an oncologist, developed an imagery technique designed to help his cancer patients take some control over their circumstances by mentally participating in their treatment. Rather than asking patients to imagine cancer cells with biological accuracy, Dr. Simenton urged people to symbolically represent their disease in any form that made sense to them. The cancerous cells might look like cauliflower or a piece of hamburger meat. Radiation treatment became a beam of "energy bullets," shooting down to kill the cancer. Healthy white blood cells could be pictured as an army of polar bears completely devouring the dead cancer debris. His patients continually imagined these symbols interacting, in a scenario that led to the defeat of the disease. The positive results of his patients in Corpus Christi, Texas, made him a national authority on mind-body interaction.

You can adapt this concept of symbolic imagery to work with positive and negative personality characteristics. The key is to first associate specific attitudes with appropriate symbols, and then design a script that has these symbols engaged in "battle," with the chosen characteristic emerging victoriously. As you repeatedly envision this interaction, you can expect a corresponding shift in attitude.

When one of my clients decided to strengthen her positive attitude, especially as it related to the way she approached workplace change, she chose to symbolize optimism as a Don Quixote figure. Her resistance to change was represented by a rigid windmill. Daily, she played out an imaginary interaction in which the man of La Mancha valiantly charged the windmill. The successful outcome was always Don Quixote's victory. As a further reminder, she purchased a small statue of Don Quixote and placed it on her desk.

In the past, this woman felt discouraged and overwhelmed whenever she had surveyed the changes going on in her company. With the help of Don Quixote, she felt fortified and empowered. She eventually found that her new attitude had a powerful impact on her entire work team, and that together, the team could contribute to and support organizational change. She saw where her efforts really made a difference.

William James said, "Human beings, by changing the inner attitudes of their minds, can change the outer aspects in their lives."

The Only Solution

A favorite story of mine is about a suburban householder whose problem was that his entire yard was covered with dandelions. He did not like these dandelions, so he tried every formula of eradication he could find. He grubbed and he sprayed and he pulled and he cut, but still he had a yard of dandelions.

Finally, in desperation, he wrote the U.S. Department of Agriculture and narrated in detail his fruitless operations—mechanical, biological and chemical. The answer came from Washington: "There is only one thing left to do. You must learn to love dandelions."

There may not be much you can do about how things are changing in your organization. But you have total control over your attitude regarding the change.

Positive Practice

Lost tourist in New York: "How do I get to Carnegie Hall?" Native New Yorker: "Practice."

How do you get to be more optimistic? The same way you get to Carnegie Hall.

Seeing positive aspects to things that you normally consider negative can open up new connections and perspectives. Practice your positive thinking skills and come up with several answers to each of the questions listed below.

♦ What are at least five positive things about getting a flat tire in the middle of rush hour traffic? *a lot of people around to help or call u help*
♦ What are at least five positive things about missing a first aid class that you need as a job requirement?
♦ What are at least five positive things about having an obnoxious boss? *— learn to accept it*
♦ What are at least five positive things about your last "bad" experience?
♦ What are at least five positive things about your most current worry?

A CHECKLIST

☐ Am I basically an optimist?

☐ Is my first reaction to an announced change to look for the opportunities?

☐ Do I "label" events in ways that promote the advantages?

☐ Can I find the positive aspects in even the most negative changes?

☐ Can I list changes in my life that started out negatively and ended up positively?

☐ Do I like challenge and change?

☐ Do I know that it is to my advantage to focus on the positive aspects of change?

☐ Do I surround myself with positive, supportive people?

Chapter 4   COPING

"I learned to deal with tremendous amounts of change by being realistic about what I could and couldn't control."

—Manager, A.T.&T.

"We can laugh about this or we can cry. I prefer to laugh."

—Consultant

Two of the most difficult aspects of change are its *complexity and accelerating pace*. This was clearly depicted by the employee who told me, "I feel like a juggler with a crazed assistant. She keeps throwing balls at me and I have to juggle faster and faster. Then, just as I get all the balls in the air, she throws in objects I've never seen before."

Many organizational changes are instigated by circumstances beyond our control: increased competition, sharp economic swings, government regulations, consumer pressures, new technologies, changing demographics, and further globalization of the marketplace. Even upper management has little or no control over these forces. The best any of us can hope to do is to adapt to the new environment as quickly and effectively as possible. Not to adapt, not to change, is professional suicide—for an individual, an organization, an industry, or a political system.

As with any other change-adept characteristic, some people are naturally good at coping. These adaptive, flexible individuals know intuitively when and how to "go with the flow" of change. Other people need help developing their coping skills.

How To Succeed While Lying Down On The Job

Two men who seemed equally qualified applied for the same job of felling trees in a forest. Since there was only one opening, the foreman proposed a test. "I want each of you to begin chopping trees at opposite ends of this grove. At the end of the day, the one who has cut down the most trees will win the job." The men agreed and set out for the grove.

The first man worked extremely hard, going straight through the day without stopping. The second man also worked at a steady pace, but once every hour he would take a five-minute break. At the end of the day both men reported to the foreman. When their results were compared, the second man was awarded the position. As they walked away, the first man could not hide his frustration. "I don't understand it. I worked straight through the day, while you sat down for five minutes every hour. How could you win?" The second man grinned. "Maybe it's because whenever I rested, I was also sharpening my axe."

Employees who have well-developed coping strategies know *they are working smarter instead of harder*. Coping strategies include time and stress management techniques, the use of humor, flexibility, and getting a "big picture" perspective of change.

Another crucial coping skill is the ability to focus—to ignore all other issues and become totally involved with the present situation. Peter Thigpen, a top executive at Levi Strauss, equates today's hectic business climate to white water rafting. "In stretches of green water, when things are relatively calm, there is time to plan and reflect. You'd better take advantage of it, because in the white water turbulence it is absolutely essential to concentrate completely on the task at hand."

Managing Time

Basically, there are two kinds of activities vying for our attention: the urgent and the important. In times of change and chaos, it is easy to get so wrapped up in the "fire fighting" aspects of your job that you neglect activities that are most important to your goals and objectives. Virtually every change-adept employee that I interviewed works from some kind of daily "to do" list. On that list, important activities are written and prioritized. Even large-scale change can be broken into manageable smaller pieces, to be prioritized and approached one step at a time.

Time management experts have been helpful in offering the following advice:

- **There are only *five options* to help you break the work-time dilemma**: 1) reduce your wasted time; 2) improve your methods; 3) delegate work to others; 4) work longer; 5) lower your expectations for results. It is up to you to choose which you want to do.
- **Set priorities and stick to them.** If you get into the habit of writing your daily list at night just before you go to bed, or at the end of each workday, you will awaken with a sense of organization and clarity. Resolve not to do things that do not help you achieve your goals. Try making a *not-to-do* list, to help remind you *not* to waste time on unimportant activities.
- **Work on one thing at a time.** Schedule your number one priority activity for first thing in the morning. Put all other projects and distractions out of sight. Stay with your top priority activity until it is completed, then cross it off your list and proceed to the next most important item. Continue through the list in this manner. Be sure to include any unfinished activities on the next day's list.
- **Reduce interruptions and work in blocks and quality time.** Identify your prime time, the time of day when you are at your peak. Make sure this is used for important work—close the door to your office, have your secretary screen all calls and delay everything possible. If you do not have a private office, go to the company library or even stay home to insure uninterrupted chunks of work time.
- **Learn to utilize time more efficiently.** Double up on "empty" duties, like listening to self-help or educational cassette tapes while driving to work or washing the dishes. In your scheduling, allow extra time for unexpected things you cannot control. Postpone trivialities, delegate whenever possible, and handle items of similar categories—

phone calls or correspondence—in blocks of time. Reward yourself for completing worthwhile activities.

Flight or Fight

The mechanism which allows our bodies to handle emergencies has come to be known as the *flight or fight response*. As danger is perceived, the brain stimulates the kidneys to release two sets of hormones: Glucocorticoids increase the level of fats, cholesterol, cortisone and sugar in the system. Extra glucocorticoids give us the energy required to face a dangerous situation. Adrenaline increases the heart rate and, consequently, the body's oxygen consumption.

As this psycho-physiological process continues, blood pressure rises and breathing becomes rapid and shallow. Blood is pumped to large muscles and away from smaller vessels; muscle tension increases, as does perspiration needed to cool the active body. Pupils dilate and the senses of hearing and smell become acute. Brain waves elevate as attention and alertness increase.

When the danger has passed, the parasympathetic nervous system reverses the bodily effects to regain equilibrium—homeostasis. As long as you experience episodic stress—those stressful situations which are specific and infrequent—you can rely on your body to discharge physical tension and automatically rebound in this manner.

You may have noticed this process working for you. If you have ever narrowly avoided an automobile accident, you probably pulled safely to the side of the road with your heart racing and your muscles tensed for anticipated action. Then, assured that you have escaped unharmed, you took a deep breath and began to release built-up tension as your body regulated its functions back to normal.

While episodic stressors allow an automatic adjustment to equilibrium, many of our stressors today are continual, anticipatory, symbolic and even imaginary. And yet, inappropriate as it may be, for all of these modern stressors we still fully gear up to physically fight or flee.

Change brings stress that accelerates and is ongoing. Without any clear signal that the *danger* is over, we rarely release the accumulated tension and allow ourselves to return to homeostasis—physically, mentally or emotionally.

The High Cost of Stress

When you add all the frustrations, conflicts and pressures we have to contend with every day, it is no wonder that each year the statistics on stress-related illness climb higher and higher:

- *Cardiovascular disease* is responsible for nearly one million deaths per year—amounting to 52 percent of deaths from all causes. (American Heart Association, *Heart Facts*)
- About 34 million Americans have *high blood pressure*. (American Heart Association, *We're Putting Our Heart Into Your Health*.)
- Americans *consume* nearly 15 tons of *aspirins* daily. (Dr. Roger Williams, author of "Nutrition Against Disease.")
- One out of every six Americans takes some form of *tranquilizer* regularly. (U.S. Committee on Drug Abuse.)
- One million people per day are *absent from work*. (Institute for the Advancement of Health, San Francisco.)

Systematic Relaxation

Relaxation techniques help reduce residual stress by promoting voluntary control over some central nervous system functions associated with arousal. By altering your breathing and releasing muscle tension, you can decrease oxygen consumption, heart rate, metabolism and brain wave activity. The more relaxation is induced, the more it will carry over into your general resistance to the harmful effects of stress.

A simple relaxation technique begins with inhaling slowly and deeply through your nose, holding your breath at the top of the inhalation, then gently exhaling through your mouth. Let your mind focus on your breathing, allowing each exhalation to carry out tension from one part of your body. With your eyes closed, start at the top of your head and become aware of any tension. As you exhale, deliberately release the tension—imagine it melting, evaporating, or draining away.

Take your time, progressing through your body until you have created a warm flow of relaxation, from the top of your head to the tips of your toes, Encourage your body to feel completely limp and slightly heavy. Pay attention to these enjoyable sensations, and store them in your memory. In this way you can recreate the feelings faster, and learn to relax yourself quickly at will. Take a few deep breaths, imagining energy being drawn in through the soles of your feet and traveling all the way up your body. Open your eyes and stretch.

Yellow Lights

The first symptoms of the *negative effects of stress* may include low energy, indigestion, disturbance of sleep patterns, and tense muscles that often result in body pains or headaches. Psychologically, an overly stressed person finds it increasingly difficult to maintain objectivity, and has trouble perceiving alternatives. This is often accompanied by a sense of pressure—not enough time, too many demands, or feelings of being trapped. The arousal of negative emotions results in poor overall performance and decision-making ability.

The first step to good stress management is to become more aware of precisely how the negative effects of stress manifest in your mind and body. In general, the following symptoms should be recognized as signals to back off and take care of yourself, not to push ahead:

Physical	Mental
Headaches	Anxiety
Muscle aches	Irritability
Digestive problems	Poor concentration
Insomnia	Depression
Accident proneness	Apathy, lethargy
Increased heart rate	Confusion, poor decisions
Fatigue	Procrastination
Appetite change	Distrust
Weight change	Instability
Rash	Nervous laugh
Minor illnesses	Loss of meaning, direction
Teeth grinding	Easily discouraged
Pain in lower back and neck	Inability to get organized
Trembling, tics, nervous habits	Spacing out, whirling mind, no new ideas

The Great Escape

Many people who feel overwhelmed by stress find destructive ways to cope. Some escape into increased use of drugs, alcohol, nicotine or food. Others withdraw socially and seek refuge in excessive hours of sleep.

Change-adept people find *productive releases* for their tension. They recognize the first signals of stress overload and utilize *personal methods* of releasing it: They take a break, vary their undertakings, breathe deeply, daydream, exercise, read, get a massage, listen to music, cry, laugh, practice relaxation techniques, or surround themselves with supportive people with whom they can talk through their feelings.

What are some of the strategies you have developed for dealing with your first sign of stress overload? What are some additional coping methods you would like to try?

Mental Vacation

A mental vacation is easier, faster, cheaper and almost as beneficial as the real thing. In a matter of minutes you can transport yourself, through your imagination, to your favorite vacation spot. Vividly recalled from reality, or created purely in your fantasy, this mental exercise influences your brain and central nervous system in ways similar to an actual experience.

- ◆ **Choose a favorite place for relaxation.** Remember, there are no limitations on your fantasy. Travel first class and arrive at the perfect time of year when the temperature is ideal. Just close your eyes and let your mind create the perfect vacation.
- ◆ **Use your five senses.** The closer you come to mentally replicating an actual experience—with visual, auditory, tactile, olfactory and gustatory input—the more potent the imagery becomes.
- ◆ **Include emotions.** As you become more and more engrossed in your fantasy, allow the accompanying emotions to intensify. Feel totally relaxed, safe, pampered and comfortable.
- ◆ **Plan your return.** As you gently come out of this pleasant state of mind, notice how good you feel. You are ready to return to reality, re-energized, refreshed and renewed.

A Diamond is a Chunk of Coal Made Good Under Pressure

The process of change and growth requires the ability to manipulate stress. While some people burn out under pressure, others *use stress to get energized*. To them, stress is the spice of life.

Stress is basically a response, a flow of energy, if you will. The only truly stress-free people are dead. A certain amount of stress is necessary to be alive. More stress is needed to move out of boredom. Added stress is necessary for top performance. Positive stress increases motivation and productivity to a point. When it becomes distress, the negative consequences begin to take effect.

Distress is a chronic, unabated triggering of the stress response, without discharge. Bad stress can also be triggered by feelings that one's decisions are useless, that life is out of control. In fact, research shows that the most detrimental work situation is one in which high stress—increased work load—combines with low control—over how, and at what rate, the work is accomplished. In those cases, there is an increase in the central nervous system's hormone production and a decrease in the dysfunction of the auto-immune system. On the other hand, high stress, coupled with high control, shows no CNS increase and no damage to auto-immunity.

Eustress

Eustress is the term coined to label positive stress, which can heighten productivity, creativity and enjoyment of life. Good stress is enhanced by a feeling of confidence and a sense of control over one's destiny.

Dean Tjosvold, professor of organizational behavior at Simon Fraser University's School of Business Administration, found that problem solvers work most constructively when confronted with serious, but not critical issues. At these moderate stress levels, people are more apt to weigh alternatives, solicit opposing points of view, and invite constructive controversy.

When faced with a full-blown crisis, however, even experienced professionals can slip, grasp for quick-fix solutions or take the path of least resistance—anything to bring an end to uncomfortable high-stress levels. Similarly, people dealing with problems they perceive as minor do not put forth their best efforts. Under low-stress conditions, the temptation is to ignore the problem or apply pat solutions. What is clear, according to Tjosvold, is that too much or too little stress can stymie effective decision making, while moderate amounts of stress can help.

Everyone has had experiences in which their performance was exceptional. While these situations are referred to in various ways—"I was on a roll." "It was a kind of flow where everything I did was just right."—peak performances are never stress-free states, but rather states in which the stress level at that time was optimal for you to achieve outstanding results.

Change-adept achievers generate the necessary amount of stress which, for them, assures maximum performance. They are aware of the first signals of *stress overload* and do not push themselves beyond those limits. Rather, they utilize effective stress-reduction techniques to release excess tension.

Craig Finney, at California State University at Northridge, has shown that employees who take voluntary breaks from tough assignments will outperform those who do not. The form of the break is not important. Some employees close their eyes and take deep breaths, some get a cup of coffee, others take a walk or do crossword puzzles. The key is that the employees are in control of the timing of their schedule and of the content of their breaks.

As the English essayist Walter Pater once said, "To burn always with this hard, gem-like flame, to maintain this ecstasy, is success in life." That is also an example of thriving on eustress.

STRESS DIET

Breakfast
½ grapefruit
1 slice whole wheat toast
8 oz. skim milk

Lunch
4 oz. lean broiled chicken breast
1 cup steamed zucchini
1 Oreo cookie
Herb Tea
Midafternoon Snack
Rest of the package of Oreos
1 quart Rocky Road ice cream
1 jar hot fudge
Dinner
2 loaves garlic bread
Large pepperoni and mushroom pizza
Large pitcher of beer
Entire frozen cheesecake eaten directly from the freezer

Flexibility

I was speaking for an insurance company in Regina, Saskatchewan. A man from the audience approached me at the break saying, "I like your point about the need to be flexible in dealing with change. I thought you might be interested in what my father discovered when he was the head of the Canadian prison system. He called it *the mark of the criminal mind*. He developed a simple test in which a prisoner would sit in a chair behind a table. On the table were two lights: a red one and a green one. When the red light shown, the prisoner was to touch the red light, and when the green light was turned on, the prisoner was to touch the green light. So far there was no problem. Everyone could perform that simple task. The trouble came whenever the red light was momentarily turned on, then quickly turned off and the green light was turned on. It seemed that once the prisoner had committed to the action of touching one or the other light, he could not change direction. Of course, you must remember that my dad was testing only the criminals who were caught. These were the same men who had decided to rob a bank at 2:00 pm, and when a police car pulled up at 1:55 pm, the robbers weren't flexible enough to change their plans. So naturally they ended up in prison."

How flexible are you? How quickly can you adapt to a new management system or product line, or to a new position within the organization? Do you realize that *flexibility is one of the* most valuable coping skills you can develop?

The Wisdom To Know the Difference

You do not have to like change to excel in changing times, but you do have to accept it and, at some point, choose to make it work. Some changes you can influence or control.

Some changes are inevitable and must be accepted as a *given*. Many people are blessed with wisdom to know when to fight and when to accept. For the rest of us, here are a series of questions devised to help make that distinction:

- ◆ What do you not like about the change?
- ◆ Do you have a better idea?
- ◆ Do you have the power or authority to present your idea?
- ◆ Do you have a safe place to vent your feelings?
- ◆ Are you willing to make this change succeed?
- ◆ If so—what are you willing to do?
- ◆ What attitude would you need to adopt to make it palatable?
- ◆ Can you change the change enough, maybe in the implementation, to make it yours?
- ◆ How can you position this change to your advantage?
- ◆ If you choose not to support this change, should you leave the company?

Just For Laughs

Many change-adept people consider *humor and fun* to be requisites of change survival. They encourage others to *lighten up*. As the president of a title insurance company said to me, "In this business, you'd better have a sense of humor."

He is not alone in his thinking. Robert Half International surveyed vice presidents and personnel directors of 100 large companies. Eighty-four percent of those interviewed thought that people with a sense of humor do a better job than those with little or no humor. Employees who could laugh and have fun were most likely to be labeled creative and flexible.

Laughter is a natural tension reducer. Dr. William Fry of Stanford University Medical School refers to it as *inner jogging*. As you laugh, you distract attention and stimulate the brain to release endorphins, the body's natural morphine-like substance. As the laughter subsides, muscles of the body go limp. Relaxation benefits last up to forty-five minutes.

Change offers plenty of reasons to be upset, worried and confused. A first line supervisor at a manufacturing company going through its third restructuring in as many years, said to me: "Things are often so confused and emotional around here that I could laugh or I could cry. I usually choose to laugh. Crying may be soothing, but laughter is healing."

If laughter is healing and helpful for dealing successfully with change, then all of us need to take stock of our "humor inventories." *What about you?*

- ◆ Who makes you laugh? (Friends, comedians, authors, cartoonists, etc.)
- ◆ What is the silliest thing you have ever done?

- What is your favorite joke?
- When was the last time you had a good laugh?

Perspective

Changes are made at corporate levels for a variety of reasons, most—or all—of which have nothing to do with your productivity or talent. Change is going on in businesses around the world. It is not a reflection of your personal worth. You can depersonalize change if you broaden your perspective to see change within a global framework.

A change of perspective can alter almost any experience. My favorite example of that process is in this letter from a college student mailed to her parents:

Dear Mom and Dad,

You've probably been wondering why I haven't written lately. I didn't want you to worry, so I hope that someone else didn't tell you about my dormitory burning down.

I was in the hospital for only a few days, and as soon as all the bandages come off, the doctors assure me that my eyesight will return to almost normal.

Luckily I found another place to stay right away. The nicest guy from a motorcycle gang let me stay with him and his friends.

I know how you've always wanted to be grandparents, so you'll be happy to hear that the baby is due in about seven months. Since I'm flunking out of school anyway, I should be home with you by then.

Your loving daughter,
Lori

P.S.

None of the above is true. The dorm is fine, my eyesight is perfect, and I'm not pregnant. In fact, I don't even have a boyfriend yet. I'm not flunking out of school, but I did get a "D" on my last French test, I'm not doing too well in my statistics class, and I could use another $200.

I just wanted to make sure that when you got this news, you'd receive it with the proper perspective.

A CHECKLIST

☐ I use my sense of humor to help cope with change.

☐ I have a broad perspective of change and the *big picture* at work.

☐ I work well under pressure.

☐ I am flexible and adapt well to change.

☐ I focus my attention on those aspects of change that I can influence or control.

☐ I accept change as a *given*.

☐ I have good time management skills.

☐ I have good stress control skills.

Chapter 5 < COUNTERBALANCE

"My goal is to achieve wholeness and balance."
—Manager, Pacific Bell

*"It is crucial to have a support system, especially
for the person out here on the limb alone."*
—President, Interactive Financial Services

One definition of the word compensate is "to provide with a counterbalance or neutralizing device." Change-adept individuals *compensate for the demands and pressures of business-related* change by developing *counterbalance* in other areas of their lives: well-defined health care practices that build resilience, outside interests that are personally fulfilling, and ongoing emotional support.

In contrast to these resilient, peak performers, the average employed person is out of balance. This is especially true in businesses where white-collar workers are working much more than a 40-hour week. Employees who regularly work excessive hours may do so out of necessity, or they may be workaholics. Perfectionism, compulsiveness and obsessiveness are traits which complement the workaholic personality. Workaholics are addicted to continually putting in long hours. It is important to realize that workaholics are not change-adept and are not peak performers. Rather, they are those employees who suffer from job "burn-out," and often end their career by getting fired.

Because change-adept employees *can enjoy both work and play*, they are more effective workers—more likely to be top performers. The following comparisons point out the differences between workaholics and employees with high counterbalance:

Workaholic	Counterbalance
Works long hours	Works regular hours
Works to keep busy	Works toward major goals
Cannot delegate	Delegates regularly
Misses vacations	Takes and enjoys vacations
Grabs a sandwich at desk	Leaves workplace for lunch
Has shallow relationships	Has deep friendships
Often misses family functions	Gives time and energy to family priorities
Has no interest outside work	Has interests and hobbies
Neglects health	Exercises and takes good care of health

Always has to keep busy working	Enjoys both work and leisure activities
Achieves much	Achieves more
Burns out	Thrives

Counterbalance Questionnaire

FOOD FOR THOUGHT

1. *How many cups of coffee, tea or caffeinated soft drinks do you consume per day?*   None
   Although studies vary in their findings, it is most often agreed that intake should be limited to three or less caffeinated beverages daily.

2. *Do you eat breakfast?*   yes
   In complete agreement with what your mother always told you, nutritionists point out the value of a healthful first meal.

3. *How many alcoholic beverages do you drink per day?*   1 or less
   It has been reported that people who have one drink per day are healthier than those who drink more or less.

4. *Are you aware of current nutrition and diet recommendations?*
   Recommendations in dietary goals come from the American Heart Association, the American Diabetes Association, and a United States Senate Committee headed by George McGovern. They include:

   ✓ Reducing total fat consumption to 30 percent of total caloric intake—achieved by cutting back on dairy products, fried foods, oils and meat
   ✓ Replacing saturated fats with unsaturated fats
   ✓ Reducing salt and sugar usage
   ✓ Increasing consumption of fruits, vegetables and complex carbohydrates—whole grains, cereals, legumes, potatoes and pasta

5. *Are you within five pounds of your ideal?*
   Unlike developing countries whose populations display diseases of under-nutrition—tuberculosis, respiratory infections, dysentery, etc.—Americans, suffer from conditions adversely affected by over-consumption—heart disease, cancer, cirrhosis of the liver and high blood pressure.

6. *Do you eat regular, moderate, healthful meals?*
   For maximum health and ideal body weight, prepare moderate meals that fulfill the body's nutritional requirements.

HAZARDOUS TO YOUR HEALTH

1. *Are you a nonsmoker?*   Yes

   Data from four university studies involving nearly 2,000 people was published in a special issue of the *Journal of the American Medical Association*. Devoted entirely to scientific examination of the links between smoking and disease, researchers leveled indictments against cigarettes on these counts:

   ◆ Smokers greatly increase their risk of suffering heart attacks. The more heavily they smoke, the greater the danger.
   ◆ Young women who smoke and want to become pregnant are less fertile than young women who do not smoke.
   ◆ Babies born to mothers who smoke show significantly lower birth weights than babies born to nonsmokers.

   Added to our existing knowledge about the hazards of smoking as related to cancer and emphysema, this makes a strong case for becoming and remaining a nonsmoker.

2. *Do you use safety belts while driving?*   Yes
   Using safety belts and driving at a safe speed are potential life extenders.

3. *Do you like your job?*   No
   Duke University conducted a ten-year longitudinal study of aging that showed that the number one factor leading to long life is happiness at work. Professional burnout is a stress-related problem, most often affecting high-achievers who face heavy pressures, work hard and feel their efforts and talents are not fully appreciated. On the other hand, those who love their work report that they respond positively to pressure and experience an internal sense of accomplishment.

4. *Do you have a strong social support system?*
   Scientific evidence suggests that having a strong social support system may be essential, in the long run, to your health and well-being. A program begun in 1982 by the California Department of Mental Health shows that:

   ◆ People who cut themselves off from others have two to three times the risk of an early death.
   ◆ Terminal cancer strikes isolated people more often than those with close ties to others.
   ◆ The rates of mental hospitalization are five to ten times greater for divorced, separated and widowed people than for married people.
   ◆ Close family ties, good friends and even pets can increase resilience and health.

HOW DO YOU SPELL RELIEF?

1. *Do you get adequate sleep?*   Sometimes
   One of the beneficial health habits uncovered at UCLA's School of Public Health was sleeping between seven and eight hours each night.

2. *Do you have three ways of unwinding that do not include drugs, alcohol or food?*
   Not everyone relaxes in the same way. Here are some possibilities to consider: aerobics, swimming, biking, walking, reading, music, hobbies, sports, television, movies, meditation, massage, and soaking in a tub.

3. *Do you have a regular exercise program to which you adhere?*
   Over the past twenty years, there has been a growing interest and increasing expertise in the physiological and psychological benefits of a regular exercise program. While any exercise you enjoy can be stress-reducing, fitness experts advise people to develop and maintain flexibility, and to engage in activities classified as cardiovascular or aerobic.

   Aerobic exercises use the large muscles nonstop, in rhythmic, repetitive motion, for a minimum of twelve minutes. During this time, the heart-rate should stay within its *target zone*. To compute your target zone, subtract your age from 220 and multiply that number by 70 percent and 80 percent. If your age were 35, your heart rate should stay between 116 and 148 beats per minute. For easy monitoring, take your pulse rate for six seconds and multiply by ten.

   The recommended aerobic schedule for cardiovascular requirements is a minimum of twenty minutes—with a warm-up period previous to and a cool-down period following—three or more times a week.

   Aerobic activity includes fast walking, biking, swimming, jogging, rowing, aerobic dancing, jumping rope, or working out on a mini trampoline. It does not include jumping to conclusions, dodging issues, side-stepping responsibilities, running in circles or pushing your luck.

4. *Do you take time to reflect, to think about your values, goals and plans?*
   Change-adept achievers develop their values and goals by taking the necessary time to dream and reflect. In this way, they clarify their priorities and simplify decision-making.

EMOTIONAL SUPPORT

1. *Does your life have emotional balance and support?*
   People who handle work-related change best are not workaholics. Although they may spend long hours at the office, few take work with them, and fewer still routinely work on weekends. Instead, they schedule pleasurable activities: sports, travel, reading, theatre, concerts, social gatherings, family events and hobbies.

A Piece of the Rock

Those who thrive on change recognize and rely on the counterbalance of emotional support, whether they find it in their family, friends, peers, religion, personal ethics or a combination of these. People I interviewed called this stability their *anchor* or their *rock*.

Relevant quotes from my research included the following: "I can go through enormous amounts of change as long as there is one person in my chain of command I can rely on." "My stability comes from my relationship with God." "I get my strength from my church group." "My family is always there for me." "It's my close circle of friends. That's what I can count on." "I would have gone nuts if I hadn't had my exercise program." "I find an anchor within myself . . . my own set of guiding principles."

The most memorable example I ever heard was from the chief executive officer of a cellular telephone company. "I've got one of those 'rocks' in my life," he reported to me. "It's my sock drawer." As I looked rather surprised, he hastily continued, "I mean it. All hell can be breaking loose at work, but when I come home at night I open my sock drawer to find everything in color-coded, neat little piles. I tell you, it does my heart good."

So, I guess it does not matter if it sounds silly to someone else—as long as it works for you. The important thing is to *identify your source of support and cultivate it.* It might also be a good idea to have more than one source of support.

The other day, an audience member approached me after I gave a speech for the International Association of Business Communicators. "You have just cleared up a great mystery for me. There is a woman on my staff who had always done so well with change, but lately was resisting every little thing. I just realized that her stabilizing force has always been her family, and that last month was the first time that both her children left home to go away to school. She's lost her only anchor."

Demographics

The influx of women into the labor force over the past 25 years has changed the demographics of the office, as well as the basic structure of the American family. Dual-income families, where both husband and wife work, are prevalent today. Dual-career marriages, where both partners are pursuing separate careers, are on the rise. The norm has changed from a family predominately headed by the husband as breadwinner, with wife and children at home, to one in which both husband and wife are employed, or to a family headed by a single parent.

Demographic trends show that employees of the 1990s bring with them a set of family responsibilities that involve not only working spouses, but also children, stepchildren, non-custodial children and elderly parents. Most individuals strive to create a balance between home and work life. This balance is not always easy to maintain, and people are not always successful in *dividing* themselves equally.

The other day I overheard the following conversation at the checkout stand in my grocery store:

Child: Why didn't Daddy have dinner with us last night?

Mother: Well honey, Daddy had a lot of work to do, so he stayed later at the office.

Child: Why did Daddy leave so early this morning?

Mother: He still hadn't finished that work at the office, so he wanted to get an early start.

Child: Maybe they could just put him in a slower group.

The Balancing Act

Most people achieving a balance between rewarding careers and invigorating personal lives are not doing it by making drastic career changes or dropping out to open bed and breakfast inns or starting their own cookie businesses. Instead, they are making less dramatic shifts such as requesting a more flexible work schedule, unconventional work sites and arrangements—such as work at home—time off for family matters, and child/elder care.

In spite of your best laid plans for a balanced life, many business-related changes require extra time and effort. Start-ups, lengthy travel periods and project deadlines can all take time away from those people and things that give and maintain our counterbalance.

Rather than trying to be a "superperson"—one who is totally balanced at all times—you will handle change best if you acknowledge that there are various cycles when one part of life—by necessity—takes precedence over another. As the Director of the Boston Advertising Club, Elizabeth Cook McCabe said, "You can have it all, but not all at once."

A certified public accountant friend of mine knows when her busiest season is. Since she has learned from past experience that there will be many weeks of extremely long workdays, she prepares for this by discussing the upcoming period with her husband and children. Her family discusses various options. They know that this will be a time when everyone will have to help out around the house, when family outings are out of the question, and when "mom" is going to be very busy. Sometimes the family decides to spend extra time together before the rush begins. Sometimes they plan a vacation for immediately after the hectic period. By facing the facts and looking at ways to compensate later, my friend can still maintain an overall counterbalance in her life.

Balancing Goals

One of the first steps to creating a more balanced life is to be sure that you have developed goals in each important area. Life/work planning consultants advocate goal setting in six areas of your life. These six areas are: physical, intellectual, social, spiritual, family and financial.

How balanced is your wheel of life?

PHYSICAL

INTELLECTUAL   FINANCIAL

SOCIAL   FAMILY

SPIRITUAL

A CHECKLIST

☐ Have I set goals in all important areas of my life?

☐ What disciplines do I need to develop to improve or maintain my health and wellness?

☐ Am I doing all I can to develop my intellectual talents and potential?

☐ Am I keeping up with what I need to know in my field?

☐ Do I recognize and cultivate a stabilizing force in my life?

☐ Am I developing myself spiritually by studying, reading, meditating and/or praying?

☐ Is the quality of my home and family life all that I would have it be?

☐ What goals have I set for my social life—my social activities and time with close friends?

☐ Are my work life and my private life in balance?

Chapter 6 < CREATIVITY

"I'm best at finding creative solutions to problems."
—Executive, Ortho Diagnostic Systems

"If you can outguess the direction of change and get there first, change becomes an incredible opportunity."
—Manager, Pacific Bell

The Competitive Edge

Innovation and creativity are quickly becoming the keys to corporate productivity and individual excellence. Former president of Quaker Oats, Ken Mason stated, "I am not impressed with the power of company presidents. I am impressed with the power of ideas."

Change-adept professionals are creative. They are curious and innovative, constantly seeking ways to improve a product, a service or themselves. They typically contribute beyond the limits of their job descriptions—to other functions, to other departments, and to the organization as a whole. They actively solicit diverse opinions that generate new thoughts, and they value any experience that exposes them to new knowledge and skills. One entrepreneur summed this up nicely when he said: 'If this venture fails, it will still be worth all the time and effort I've put into it for the past eighteen months. Just look at everything I've learned!"

Out of the Mouths of Babes

In the late 1940s, a group of psychologists were discussing the lack of creativity in most adults. They speculated that by the age of 45, there was only a minute percentage of the population who could think creatively. To prove their assumption they tested a group of 45-year-olds. They found less than 5 percent of them to be creative.

As the psychologists continued testing, the age of the subjects went down to forty, thirty-five, thirty, twenty-five, twenty years old. The 5 percent figure stayed accurate. Finally, at seventeen years old, the percentage rose to 10 percent, and at the age of five it jumped to over 90 percent. Although many of us would label ourselves *not very creative*, almost all of us were highly creative at five.

Developing your innate creative potential is a gift to your organization, to your co-workers, and especially to yourself. You begin to break the barriers of self-doubt, preconceived values, and habits that block the creative flow when you, first of all, accept the fact that you already are creative. You just need a little guidance to help you on your journey to richer and more innovative ways of thinking.

School Daze

Instead of encouraging the natural creative aptitude in all five-year-olds, modern education seems to squelch creativity. Children are put in groups and made to sit at desks and raise their hands before they talk. All the emphasis is on conformity and order. Along with their ABCs, children are also taught the following lessons:

1. There is only one right answer.
2. Failure is bad.
3. Conform to the group.
4. Follow all the rules.
5. There is always a logical solution.

Regardless of how well those tenets may have served you in school, the guidelines for creative problem-solving in business challenges the validity of everything you were previously taught. Here are the new lessons:

1. There are multiple right answers.

Highly creative people know the value of going beyond one right answer to another, and still another, possibility. An effective manager who leads staff brainstorming sessions told me, "I believe in what Linus Pauling said, 'The best way to get good ideas is to have lots of ideas.' I can't afford to stop at the first right answer."

In some professions, people have spent years finding the right way to do their jobs. When those folks are confronted with the philosophy of Kaizen—the quality concept of continuous improvement—it can feel like a personal attack requiring an admission that their past performance was inadequate. They will resist the concept of improvement because, they figure, once you have found the right way to do your job, why should you ever change it?

Of course, as a professional you should cultivate a thorough knowledge and understanding of basic principles within your own field, but do not let your expertise become a block to new approaches and concepts that come from outside your field. In fact, learnings in many fields can help you stretch your horizons and see creative connections.

One of the hardest lessons for many professionals to learn is that there are multiple right ways to do business—multiple right ways to deliver health care or pizza or a joke. Your past efforts may indeed be one right way to do your job, but it is not necessarily the only right way. Continuous improvement is the process by which current *right ways* can grow into even more effective *right ways*.

In the same context, I no longer have to be wrong for you to be right and you do not have to be wrong for me to be right. We can both be right. From a field of multiple right answers, we may choose to implement your solution, because it is more cost effective or timely, or because it fits best within our mission; that does not necessarily make my solution wrong.

2. Failure is good.

Innovation is the practical result of creative ideas. From ideas come new products, systems or processes. Just as innovation requires creativity, creativity necessitates risk. And risk brings failure. Without failure, there is no innovation. Period.

Tom Watson, Sr., the founder of IBM, has often been quoted as saying, "The way to accelerate your success is to double your failure rate." Author Tom Peters declares that the prescription for dramatically speeded-up organization innovation is dramatically increased rates and amounts of failure.

"Failure is not a crime. Failure to learn from failure is." Or so said Walter Wriston, the former chairman of Citicorp. Before people can learn from failure, they must acknowledge it. The *Three "Rs"* Technique is a tool to help people learn quickly from their failures:

First R—Review: mentally go over the failure and the behaviors leading up to it. Examine the failure carefully, extracting any lesson of value.

Second R—Redo: using the feedback from part one, decide if a corrective course of action is possible. If so, make plans to implement it. If not, ask yourself, "Knowing what I know now about the outcome, how could I have handled this better? If I had it to do over, what would I change?" Allow the possibilities and strategies to form an image of a potentially more successful approach. Mentally file this solution, for future reference.

Third R—Release: the final step is the most important. Let go of the failure. Release it mentally, and emotionally detach from it. Your inner worth is not dependent on this one decision or performance. You are still a capable, resourceful, talented professional with limitless creative potential.

3. Cultivate diverse perspectives.

If you and I are in a problem-solving session, and we think alike, one of us is redundant. An exercise I often use in team-building programs involves a grid of sixteen puzzles. I allow two minutes for people to try to solve the puzzles by themselves, then I give them time with other team members to finish the exercise. Before they team up, I ask: "What is it that you want from the other team members?" Without fail, the answer comes back, "I want from them the solutions that I don't already have."

That is what we all need from other members of our teams. We need perspectives, insights and solutions that we do not already have. We do not need conformity. We need creative collaboration. Conformity is what the training film *Brain Power* refers to as *collective igno-*

rance. On the other hand, collaboration is the process of blending of diverse opinion, expertise and perspective toward a shared objective or goal. You can create a climate for collaboration by asking questions, looking for new viewpoints and valuing the creative ideas of others.

4. Continually challenge rules.

Blindly following rules encourages a mentally lazy acceptance of the status quo and is contradictory to creative thinking. To reduce your reliance on rules and policies, learn to view them as flexible guidelines, rather than iron-clad requirements. Once you feel comfortable with regulations as means rather than ends, practice breaking out of the mold in some way each week, until it becomes a habit.

The people who break free of yesterday's view of things usually begin by challenging themselves to be creative and more innovative in their own situations. You can begin by exploring your daily routine. Look at the way you typically go about your work day. What are your own "rules" of behavior?

It might be interesting to see what would happen if you broke the rules by:

♦ Taking an alternative route to work
♦ Spending your lunch hour in a totally new way
♦ Moving your desk
♦ Trying something that others would think was *totally out of character* for you
♦ Planning to spend the weekend doing something you have never done
♦ Asking somebody a "stupid" question
♦ Initiating conversation with a person whom you do not know
♦ Wandering into another part of the organization and talking with people there
♦ Signing up for a foreign language class
♦ Reading a book on a topic you've never investigated

As you review your work routine, remember that virtually nothing you do cannot be done in a slightly better, slightly different way. Success for an individual—or for an organization—may depend on how well we find new, creative solutions to the challenges of everyday life.

Here are some great questions to pose to yourself when you want to encourage originality:

✓ What would happen if . . . ?
✓ What am I assuming? How can I check whether or not these assumptions are accurate?
✓ How would someone who did not know the rules—without my expertise—view this?
✓ What do the circumstances of this problem remind me of? Is there anything in a similar situation that suggests a new way to see or do something about the current situation?

✓ What is the most outrageous solution I can create? Is there any way to modify my outrageous idea into a more workable solution?

✓ Why is that rule in place?

✓ Why not try something new?

5. Respect intuition.

When Dr. Jonas Salk became a scientist, he would picture himself as a virus or cancer cell and try to sense what it would be like to be either. Einstein proposed that imagination is more powerful than knowledge. Highly creative individuals go beyond logical problem-solving to include imagination, emotion, humor and intuition.

At the New Jersey Institute of Technology, Douglas Dean has studied the relationship between intuition and business success. His findings state that 80 percent of company executives whose companies' profits had more than doubled in the past five years had above-average precognitive powers. Weston Agor, of the University of Texas in El Paso, found that of the 2,000 managers he tested, higher-level managers had the top scores in intuition. Andrew Carnegie, John D. Rockefeller, and Conrad Hilton are examples of executives who relied heavily on their intuitive business decisions. A story about Conrad Hilton highlights the value of what was referred to as "one of Connie's hunches." There was to be a sealed bid on a New York property. Mr. Hilton evaluated its worth at $159,000 and prepared a bid in that amount. He slept that night and upon awakening, the figure $174,000 stood out in his mind. He changed the bid and submitted the higher figure. It won. The next lowest bid was $173,000. He subsequently sold the property for several million dollars.

Dr. Joel L. Moses, psychologist at AT&T corporate headquarters, was quoted in an in-house publication as saying, "Traditionally at AT&T our people are logical; they rely on numbers and data-collection techniques to solve problems, while shying away from an intuitive approach that might sometimes be more appropriate."

As the rate *of change accelerates, analysis is often too slow a tool for decision making.* Many times it is the hunch that defies logic, the "gut feeling" or the flash of subconscious insight that turns out to be the best solution. Those professionals who are both highly cognitive and highly intuitive will have a distinct advantage in solving problems.

To encourage intuition, keep a journal. A journal is not simply a record of events. Use it to keep track of ideas, observations, quotations and poems you want to remember. Write down your perceptions of trends and events, record your dreams, feelings and intuitions. Check back occasionally to see which of your hunches were accurate. By *keeping score*, you will soon learn to have faith in your intuitive perceptions.

Split Decision

In 1981, Roger Sperry was awarded the Nobel Prize for his proof of the split brain theory. According to Dr. Sperry, the two hemispheres of the brain have different, but overlapping, functions. The right and left hemispheres each specialize in distinct types of thinking processes.

With 95 percent of all right-handed people, the left side of the brain not only cross-controls the right side of the body, but is also responsible for analytical, linear, verbal and rational thought. Most left-handed people have the hemispheric functions in reverse. Balancing your checkbook, remembering names and dates, and setting goals and objectives are left-brain functions. Since many of our concepts of thinking come from Greek logic, left-brain function is most important in our educational system.

The right brain hemisphere controls the left side of the body and is holistic, imaginative, nonverbal and artistic. Whenever you recall someone's face, become engrossed in a symphony, tell a joke, or simply daydream, you are encouraging right-brain function. A young man once asked management expert Peter Drucker how to become a better manager. "Learn to play the violin," Drucker replied. He was suggesting that activities which favor the right side of the brain—whether music or woodworking, photography or dancing—will, indirectly, increase your ability to deal with people and solve business-related problems.

Swing Shift

Have you ever struggled to solve a problem and found the answer "popped" into your mind while you showered or jogged or just after you awakened? If so, you have experienced the process of releasing left-brain control to gain right-brain insight.

Singer John Denver tells how he wrote the song *Calypso*. The words to the chorus came easily to him as he was walking on the deck of Jacques Cousteau's ship. To be featured in a television special, all Denver had to do was write the verses for the song. He struggled every day. The verses would not come. The television show was filmed without the song. Later, he wanted to use the song in a concert tour. More struggle. Still the verses were not there. Finally, the singer decided that maybe the song was not meant to happen. He let go of it. Then, while skiing in Colorado he suddenly felt an urgent need to get home to work on the song. During the twenty minute drive home, the rest of *Calypso* came to him. "It was just suddenly there," according to Denver.

The president of a manufacturing company in Pennsylvania finds that he is most effective at generating new ideas when he is running. So does a vice president of marketing in California. A sales representative likes to solve problems while she sleeps. Before she retires she tells herself that she will have an answer in the morning. When she awakens, she usually has a solution in mind. A friend of mine meditates on problems. Another puts the entire situation out of his mind and tells a joke. None of these people are aware they are shifting brain hemispheres. What they do know, from trial and error, is how to get the results they want.

Whole Brain Solutions

Creative problem-solvers understand how both hemispheres of the brain—both kinds of thinking processes—complement each other. They know which function best supports each phase of the problem-solving process.

Phase One: Logically define the problem. (Left Hemisphere)

Phase Two: Generate multiple possibilities and alternative solutions. (Right Hemisphere)

Phase Three: Based on your criteria, pragmatically evaluate ideas to determine which are most applicable. (Left Hemisphere)

Phase Four: Prepare a plan for gaining support and persuading others by sharing your vision and commitment. (Right Hemisphere)

Phase Five: Prepare a plan for gaining support and persuading others by detailing savings in cost, increases in productivity, etc. (Left Hemisphere)

During the idea-generation phase, it is most important to stay in a *right brained* frame of mind. The challenge is to find ways to remain relaxed, playful, open and even silly. If you are dealing with a brainstorming group, you can begin with a warm-up exercise that will loosen up people and give them permission to be and say ridiculous and improbable things. Remember not to judge or criticize any of the ideas during idea-generation.

Plugging Into Imagination

I like this exercise in guided imagination, because it combines two right-brain functions: visualization and free association. It helps to have another person read the script to you, and lead you through the process.

1. Begin by choosing a specific problem or issue for which you would like additional insights and possibilities.

2. Give this script to the person you selected to guide you through the process. Find a comfortable position and close your eyes while your friend reads the script aloud to you.

SCRIPT

With your eyes closed, focus on your breathing. Inhale deeply and exhale fully. With each exhalation, think the word RELAX. Feel yourself releasing any physical tension as you imagine a flow of relaxation all the way down your body, from the top of your head to the tips of your toes. Allow yourself to relax deeply . . . comfortably . . . completely. Now, as I count from 10 to 1, imagine yourself on an elevator . . . a very special elevator . . . going deeper and deeper down with every number (Count slowly) 10-9-8-7-6-5-4-3-2-1. As you leave the elevator, you enter a very special room. It is your own creativity room, decorated just the way you want it to be . . . with the colors, furniture, wall decorations and equipment of your choice. You feel instantly safe and at home here. (Pause for a few seconds.) In a moment you will hear a knock on the door of your room, announcing the arrival of your creativity consultant. It may be someone you know or someone you have consciously chosen to help you. Occasionally, your consultant is subconsciously chosen, and you may be surprised when that person appears. In any event, your consultant is a symbolic representation of your creative imagination. Now, hear the knock and go to the door to greet your consultant. Open the door. (Pause for a few seconds.) Invite your consultant into the room and explain your challenging situation in full detail. (Pause for a few seconds.) Ask your consultant for any *advice or insight*. (Pause for a few seconds.) At this point you may hear your consultant speaking to you, or you may be aware of an idea or feeling that occurs to you. (Pause for a few seconds.) Ask your consultant *for a clue to solving* your problem, something that can be summarized in a single image or word. Watch and listen carefully. (Pause for a few seconds.) If you see or hear nothing, just clear your mind and let the first word you think of serve as the clue from your consultant. Don't be concerned if there is no obvious or logical connection between the image/word and your problem. Just accept whatever comes to you as having some hidden value. (Pause for a few seconds.) Now thank your consultant and lead him or her to the door. Say good-bye, and look around your room one more time. (Pause for a few seconds.) Take your image or word with you as you leave the room and enter the elevator. As I count from 1 to 10, feel yourself coming back to this present time and place. (Count slowly)

1-2-3-4-5-6-7-8-9-10. Open your eyes and write whatever word or image came into your mind.

3 Using your image/word as a stimulus, immediately write whatever thoughts come to you. Continue to free associate, writing nonstop for at least five minutes.

4 Later, as you evaluate your insights, look carefully for any pragmatic applications. The more you practice using your imagination to enhance your creativity, the more adept you will become at gathering and trusting this kind of information.

To give you one example of how this exercise can work, a nurse, fighting a serious case of burnout, after twenty-two years on the job, focused on what she would do about her work pressure. She found that her creative consultant was a wise old woman who gave her a map of the world. As the nurse free-associated around the word *map,* she realized that her job was killing her and that she could not afford to wait three years for full retirement. She acknowledged that what she really longed to do was to travel, to go new places and to have new experiences—to use her map of the world.

Clearing the Way for Creativity

Most of us have self-stifling mechanisms that we use to inhibit creative participation. Becoming aware of inhibiting habits and thought patterns can be the first step in liberating yourself from them.

Which of these have you used to hold back a creative idea?

It made me afraid.
It was a silly idea.
It was not important enough.
It was not a new idea.
Anyone could have thought it.
People probably would not like it.
It might not work.
I could not explain it right.
It was too difficult to do.
It was too bizarre an idea.
I did not know enough about the situation.

No one is exactly like you. No one sees the situation in just the same way that you do. Your contribution is unique. Your input is invaluable. When you withhold ideas for any reason, you deny yourself the opportunity to leave your mark on the world.

Continuous Improvement

You may be doing your job very well. You might even have been doing it well for years. That does not mean you can rely on the old tried-and-true approach forever. The Chief of Personnel for Toyota, the most profitable automobile company in the world, was quoted as saying: "*Our current success is the best reason to change.*"

The concept of continuous improvement begins with the acceptance that the status quo is not perfect. Creative employees tend to question everything—especially their own work habits.

✓ What work habits prevent you from doing your job better?
✓ What work procedures prevent you from doing your job better?
✓ What work systems prevent you from doing your job better?
✓ What work policies prevent you from doing your job better? What aspects of your job do you like least? What feels like a drag? What feels like "busy work"?
✓ How might any of these be improved?

The Fifteen-Minute Competitive Advantage

Woody Allen once said that he was not worried about advanced civilizations landing on earth and taking us over, because they were centuries ahead of us in technology. Instead, what worried him the most was being invaded by aliens who would be only fifteen minutes ahead. They would always be first in line for the movies and they never miss an appointment with the boss.

In a rapidly changing business environment, change-adept companies and individuals do indeed gain from the *fifteen-minute competitive advantage*—a head start on the new product line, first to apply a new concept, first to advance an innovative approach, faster at responding to the customer. Instead of waiting for the one brilliant idea that will launch their careers into super-stardom, the change-adept compete and excel with a constant stream of small improvements.

A CHECKLIST

- ☐ Do I believe that I am creative?

- ☐ Do I have confidence in my ability to solve problems creatively?

- ☐ Do I look for multiple right answers?

- ☐ Do I value the creative ideas of others?

- ☐ Do I know my own creative process—when, where and under what conditions I am most creative?

- ☐ Do I rebound from failure?

- ☐ Do I respect my business intuition?

- ☐ Do I challenge the status quo?

- ☐ Do I play with outrageous possibilities, viewing them as paths that may lead to something in the long run?

- ☐ Am I pushing myself to experiment with the daily habits and routines of my life?

- ☐ Do I embrace the philosophy of continuous improvement?

Chapter 7 — THE TRANSITION PROCESS

"All changes, even the most longed for, have their
melancholy; for what we leave behind is part
of ourselves; we must die to one life before we
can enter into another."
—Anatole France, French writer

"I'm not afraid of death. It's just that I don't
want to be there when it happens."
—Woody Allen, American actor

Beginning at the End

Change is not an event. It is a process. This process of transition or transformation begins with an ending. No matter how beautiful the butterfly may be, with its metamorphosis comes the death of a caterpillar. Change commences with the understanding that, for one thing to start, something else must be over.

Major organizational change begins with the *death* of the old organization. New management starts with the demise of old mentors and known relationships. New systems bring loss of feelings of competence that came with knowledge of the old system. Flatter organizational structures and increased employee empowerment signal the end of familiar roles and responsibilities. As soon as upper management announces a restructuring, new strategy, or launch of a new product line, you need to figure out how it changes your situation and your future. Remember that change has a ripple effect on an organization. Even those events that do not directly involve you may have some personal ramifications. A relatively minor layoff in another department may not directly affect you, but it can mark the end of the no-layoff policy that you have always taken for granted. The closing of a regional office may leave you without the clerical support you have relied on. The hiring of a new regional vice president may bring added pressure on your boss, who in turn increases your work load.

The process of change always begins with letting go of something. It may be an assumption about the rules by which you were playing, it may be a belief you held about the company or its management, or it may even be the image you held of yourself and your position within the organization. To understand the impact of changes currently facing you, start by asking yourself:

- ◆ What do I really have to let go of?
- ◆ What specifically is ending?
- ◆ What am I giving up?

The Cycle of Transition

When endings take place, people get emotional. They go through a process of grieving that is a natural sequence of emotional responses to loss. At the heart of the grieving process is sadness over what people are being asked to leave behind.

Loss hurts. It hurts employees and it hurts the company. Employees grieving over the personal impact of a change, or resentful over the loss of their colleagues, find it hard to concentrate on work. Productivity drops while accidents, illnesses and absences multiply.

Many people want to avoid these painful responses and pretend they are over them. You may find yourself in a situation where you even feel that it is foolish or wrong to feel emotional. Just know that by acknowledging your feelings at whatever stage you are in, you will move more quickly through it and on to the next phase. *The emotions of transition are denial, anger, fear and depression.* Uncomfortable as they may be, they are also the path by which you get to acceptance and commitment.

♦**DENIAL -** For many employees, the first response to announced organizational change will be denial. This is an expected initial reaction in which hurt people protect themselves from the first impact of loss. When you are experiencing this emotional stage, you feel numb and the change seems unreal. You might try to minimize the change or to ignore it completely. Typically people think:

This can't be happening.

It will all blow over. It's just a matter of time.

I don't think my job will be affected by all the changes.

♦**ANGER -** When people have moved through the numbness of denial, they may begin to feel anger at the organization. When you are angry, resentment can build. Angry employees look for places to direct blame—the company, the management, or themselves—for getting into this situation. Typical thoughts include:

I'm not going to put up with this—not without a fight.

How could I have been so stupid?

How could they do this to me? After all I've done for them!

♦**FEAR -** Fear and anxiety can rise as employees begin to doubt their ability to deal with an uncertain future. When anxiety runs high, mistakes are made, deadlines are missed. Work often grinds to a standstill for weeks. If you are afraid, you tend to pull into yourself and keep a *low profile.* One employee put it this way: "I'm keeping my head down and becoming part of the furniture." Other common thoughts include:

What will I do if I get fired?

I don't think I can learn a new system.

How am I supposed to get my work done with all these stupid changes?

♦**DEPRESSION -** Like sadness and anger, at some point feelings of depression are to be expected. Depression may be unpleasant and hard to deal with, but it is perfectly normal.

While you cannot make it go away, you can go through it and survive intact. Just remember that when you are feeling depressed, you tend to magnify the discouraging aspects of a situation. You may distort the difficulties involved with coping with the change. There is an inclination to dwell on feelings of despair and powerlessness, thinking, for example,

There's nothing I can do anyway.

I give up.

I'll never be able to trust another manager - company again.

When you recognize any of these signs of grieving in yourself, do not suppress them. Rather, look for appropriate settings in which to express your feelings. In my experience, moving through the emotional phases of change can take days, weeks or sometimes months. The more you acknowledge your feelings and get support for being in transition, the more quickly you will move through it. This is the time to take advantage of any professional counseling that your company offers. Your organization's employment assistance program (EAP) is a good place to start. If need be, seek the expertise of a pastoral counselor or a psychotherapist. A trained counselor can guide you through the stages of grieving and be a sounding board for your future plans. Believe me, you will not be alone—many of the change-adept professionals I interviewed told me they might not have gotten through traumatic changes without competent counseling.

Parting Rituals

Endings occur more easily if people can find a way to say good-bye to the past. Sometimes this means taking something tangible from the past with you into the future. When the Almaden Winery was sold, employees grieved especially for the loss of a beautiful winery rose garden where people spent lunch hours. Management noticed that employees were going into the garden and taking home rose cuttings.

During a research project on employee relocation, I discovered that relocating families found it helpful to make a formal ritual of mourning their old neighborhood before going on to the new location. They would throw themselves a *going away party*, or schedule time for the entire family to tour the area together for one last look.

Whether you make a scrapbook of your old company and co-workers, or get together with friends to fondly reminisce, the time spent honoring the past is cathartic. It can also be a healthy beginning to releasing the past.

Reframing the Ending

Whenever something is ending, it is completely normal to romanticize *the good old days*. You may notice this tendency toward *selective memory* in yourself whenever you speak of something you especially miss about the past. Once in a while, just for balance, think about things in the past that are ending that you are happy to let go of. Many professional opportunities come from looking at areas that did not work well under the old conditions, and finding ways within the new environment to improve them.

Some things are ending, but not everything is ending. A great deal is going to continue. Take stock of those constants. Are you going to be in the same facility? Is the mission of the organization still the same? Do you report to the same person? Is compensation still determined as it was before the change? What specifically is staying the same?

Going Through the Middle of Change

When people have been allowed to express their feelings and to respectfully release the past, they are ready to move on to the next phase of change. In his book, *Managing Transitions*, William Bridges refers to this phase of change as the *neutral zone*. He says that in the neutral zone "personnel are overloaded, signals are often mixed, and systems are in flux and therefore unreliable." In this chaotic, ambiguous phase, it is only natural that people become polarized between those who want to rush forward and those who want to return to the old ways.

When you are in the middle of change, you can expect to feel anxious, confused and uncertain. Things will appear worse than they were before the change, teamwork will suffer, absenteeism will rise, and company loyalty will be low. While most people think that change is a straight line from the old to the new, it is helpful to understand and anticipate the dangers and the potential opportunities inherent in the middle. Remember, this is another part of the process of change, and while it takes time, this too will pass.

In the meantime, do not overload yourself with decisions you do not have to make and with responsibilities you do not have to take on. Pace yourself. Take time out. Schedule a weekend vacation. Leave the building at lunch, and find comfortable places to dine and relax. Practice stress control techniques. Take stock of your priorities and see if they still make sense to you. Keep your sense of humor.

Temporary Structures

A graphic artist decided to leave his company and form his own free-lance operation. Although initially delighted by the idea of working out of his home, after a few weeks he found that he could not function without the structure and disciplined routine of an off-site office.

Structure is very important to many people in business. Outplacement counselors are aware that the lack of structure can demoralize the efforts of professionals looking for a job. Counselors tell their clients to set a routine: Wake up at a prescribed time, get dressed and *ready for work*. Outplacement facilities include offices or cubicles where clients come to make phone calls and set up appointments.

In the middle of any change, it may seem that all structure has fallen apart. If so, this is the time to take the initiative and to create your own temporary structure. Schedule activities that give your day a sense of order and stability. Set some short-term, achievable goals that will help you retain a feeling of accomplishment.

Most of all, while at work, focus on the job at hand. Do not allow yourself to become so distracted by the ambiguity of the situation that you stop working. Sure, you do not know exactly how it will all come out. Neither does anybody else. Focus on those things over which you have control, rather than becoming paralyzed by all the things over which you have no control.

Exploration

From a human standpoint, not all large-scale change results in less desirable conditions than what was known before. In fact, employees often find themselves with greater responsibilities and opportunities. If you can draw on your positive attitude and creative energy during this period, you will find ways to capitalize on the future. While the middle of change is by nature chaotic, it can also be exhilarating for those who explore the new possibilities ahead.

During the exploration phase, energy is released as people focus their attention on the future. In this phase, you will probably want to explore where you stand in the organization, what results need to be achieved, and what opportunities lie ahead. Now is the time to make sure you understand the new direction and vision of the organization. It is time to see where this vision aligns with your own personal values. It is also an appropriate time to take stock of your special talents and skills and see where they might fit best into the changing situation.

Management expert Peter Drucker says, "Entrepreneurs see change as the norm and as healthy. Usually they do not bring about the change themselves. But—and this defines entrepreneur and entrepreneurship—the entrepreneur always searches for change, responds to it, and exploits it as opportunity."

Right in the middle of change is the perfect time to practice your entrepreneurial skills. Treat yourself to a class in creative problem-solving. Reevaluate and redesign your work procedures. Brainstorm with your co-workers to look for new answers to old problems. Constantly challenge yourself to look for any advantages that this change affords you personally.

New Beginnings

Beginnings are psychological phenomena—another phase of the transition process. Events can start at a fixed time—the new system can be installed, the new boss can report to work, the merger can be completed—but nothing begins until people are ready to commit to the new structure, to identify with it, and to reinvest their emotional energies.

You may notice signs of acceptance within yourself: You once again *care* about the organization, and feel that your work *matters*. You feel anxious—you might think: "Even good ideas don't always work out" or, "Maybe I won't be able to keep up"—but, at the same time, feel excited that you have a chance to start something. At this point you are ready to do whatever is required to support the change.

Supporting the change fully requires that you understand the rationale behind the change, know what the new goals and objectives are, have enough information on the organization's overall plan to reach those goals, and can identify your role within that plan. It takes time and energy to gather all the necessary information, but, without that knowledge, you have only a start, not a real beginning.

All phases of transition bring pressure and stress to participants. Recognize that you are through with grieving what you have left behind. You have survived the ambiguities of the middle of change. This new beginning might be the perfect time to celebrate. Whether you host a *victory* party or splurge on a night on the town, take this opportunity to acknowledge and reward yourself.

A CHECKLIST

☐ Do I know what I am losing in this change?

☐ Can I list exactly what will be different for me?

☐ Do I know what is changing that I am happy to lose?

☐ Can I list those things that are not ending?

☐ Can I identify the signs of mourning in myself?

☐ Do I have emotional support and a safe place to express my feelings?

☐ Have I found ways to honor the past?

☐ Have I found ways to say good-bye to the past?

☐ Do I understand that it is normal to feel somewhat confused and uncertain in the middle of change?

☐ Have I created an interim structure for myself?

☐ Am I looking for creative opportunities to contribute?

☐ Do I have short-range goals that I know I can achieve?

☐ Am I taking time to relax and emotionally regroup?

☐ Am I keeping a positive mental attitude or do I need an "attitude adjustment"?

☐ Am I planning to celebrate the new beginning?

☐ Do I agree with the rationale behind the change?

☐ Do I have a clear picture of the goals and objectives of this change?

☐ Do I know what steps are required to reach these goals?

☐ Do I know what my specific role will be?

☐ Can I support the change and commit to its accomplishment?

Chapter 8 | TAKING CONTROL OF CHANGE

*"The winners of tomorrow will deal proactively
with chaos, will look at the chaos per se as the
source of market advantage, not as a problem
to be got around."*
—Tom Peters, author, **Thriving on Chaos**

*"When choosing between two evils, I always like
to try the one I've never tried before."*
—Mae West

Proactive Response to Change

In my research, I found two important ways people use their creativity to help them deal with change: *reactively and proactively*. Some people are good creative problem-solvers. They react to change with great confidence in their ability to solve whatever problems are inherent in the change.

As powerful as reactive creativity may be, the most powerful use of creativity lies in one's ability to be proactive. *Staying ahead of change*—taking a proactive approach—means anticipating the new actions that external events will eventually require. It means taking them early, before being forced to do so, while there is still time to influence or even redirect events. Karl and Steven Albrecht, in *The Creative Corporation,* write about how scientists get a spacecraft on the moon: They do not aim directly at the moon. Rather, they aim the rocket for the spot where the moon will be by the time the rocket gets there.

The very process of dealing with change proactively includes *forecasting probable changes and examining various options* in advance. At all levels of an organization, proactive people prepare themselves for upcoming events.

Several years ago, I met a young woman working in the typing pool of her company. She told me that she suspected a change was shortly going to take place in her organization. "I've been reading," she said, "and I noticed that all our competitors have automated. I'm sure it can't be very long before we, too, will require all secretarial staff to be computer-literate. You know what I'm doing? I'm not waiting for the company to train me. I'm already enrolled in computer school. When this change comes, I plan to be indispensable. If anyone's job is in jeopardy during this transition, it surely won't be mine."

While no one can be totally accurate in predicting future happenings, and no one can be 100 percent certain about increasing his or her job security, proactive employees have a distinct advantage in their mental preparation for change. When they combine this kind of *probable future* planning with an open-minded flexibility toward unknown variables, they take control of change in powerful, personally effective ways.

One Step Ahead of the Game

The following is a technique designed to help participants identify future conditions and to practice developing responses to them. I have also successfully used a form of this exercise with management teams, to create a shared vision of the direction of their organization. Have someone read the exercise to you while you follow the three simple steps:

Step #1 - With your eyes closed, take three deep breaths inhaling through your nose. Hold each breath for a count of three, then exhale through your mouth, as if you were gently pushing your exhalation across the room. Allow your body to settle into a comfortable position and release any unnecessary tension.

Step #2 - Mentally envision a calendar showing today's date. Watch the pages of the calendar flip over until months pass and finally years go by. Stop the calendar at five years from today. Add five years to your age and imagine yourself that far into the future. Pretend you are at work. What kind of company do you work for? What kind of job do you have? What were the skills and knowledge that prepared you for this job? How has this industry changed in the past five years? How has your profession changed? How have you prepared yourself to meet these challenges?

Step #3 - Stay open to any insights and ideas that just "come to you" during this exercise. When you finish, open your eyes and write a few notes on anything that seems important to you.

Forces of Change

Two major categories of forces are responsible for the vast amount of change in the workplace: *external forces*—the economy, global competition, new technology, etc.—and *internal forces*—the changing values and lifestyles of employees. While the first category brings changes that are—for the most part—imposed on participants, the second category often brings changes that are eagerly sought.

Dealing successfully with the external forces of change means facing some hard truths: Today you work for yourself. Your only *family* is your real family—not the company, and no big organization is going to take care of your future. This means that the responsibility for your success and happiness is in your own hands. You alone are in charge of clarifying your values, defining success, designing a career path, building motivation and developing a winning strategy for anticipating and capitalizing on the future.

For the change-adept, this is already standard operating procedure. Some employees never waited for their companies to *empower* them; they went right out and empowered themselves. After I presented a program for Bell Canada in Toronto, an audience member raised her hand to comment: "I'm new at this company, but there is one change that I wish we'd make. I wish we had a mentor program in the organization. To be paired with an experienced manager—to have someone to 'show us the ropes'—that would really shorten the time it takes new people to adjust." From the stage, I asked —in all my consultant's wisdom—"Well, why don't you find your own mentor?" The woman was way ahead of me. "Oh, I already did that," she replied. "I just think it would be a great program for all new employees."

For many of us, realizing that we are totally in control of our lives is traumatic. Gloria Steinem has said, "People waste more time waiting for someone to take charge of their lives than they do in any other pursuit."

I call this phenomenon the *Oz Myth*—the belief that someone wiser and more powerful than ourselves—the wizard—will provide us with solutions to our problems. Just as it was for Dorothy and her friends in the *Wizard of Oz,* it is time for all of us to look within and to realize that we can rely on our own hearts and minds and courage.

Changing Values

The term *values* refers to the *attitudes, beliefs, opinions, hopes, fears, prejudices, needs, desires and aspirations that,* taken together, govern how one behaves. One's interior set of values finds holistic expression in a lifestyle.

The values and lifestyles study (VALS) by Stanford Research Institute International (SRI) is one attempt to analyze the lives of Americans, to discover why people believe and act as they do. After studying the changing values of the workforce for over twenty years, SRI discovered that employees are becoming increasingly inner-directed. Beyond the external rewards for work, people are looking for an internal *payoff*.

Here is the profile of inner-directed employees:

- ◆ They want to be able to say, "I am a good person."
- ◆ They want jobs that are personally satisfying and rewarding.
- ◆ They care about quality-of-life and personal growth issues.
- ◆ They want to be a part of *something that matters*.
- ◆ They feel they have a right to fair and honest treatment.
- ◆ They want control over decisions that affect their lives.
- ◆ They want to identify with the values and policies of their organizations.

Values Clarification

What values are most meaningful to you?
Are you managing your time and activities to be your best self?
How do you define success in life?
How does your work fit into your definition of success?
How do you know what is or what is not ethical behavior?

These are all difficult questions that face each of us. Those who have taken the time to think through the issues and to address the ramifications of their answers, have an edge on the rest of us: They have a solid philisophical foundation upon which to base all business decisions.

Here are a few comments from employees who say they rely on clear values to guide them:

"I know exactly what I stand for and the kind of atmosphere necessary for me to fit in and to contribute. I know whether or not my personal 'culture' matches an organizational culture. This makes it easy for me to accept or refuse positions."

"I joined this company because it values the same things that I do. I appreciate and echo my organization's view of social responsibility."

"I love my work, but if I were asked to relocate I would refuse to leave the area. It would be an easy choice. I know what my priorities are; my top value is quality of life for me and my family."

Motivation

Motivation surfaces from within. Everybody motivates himself. Motivation stems from actions that satisfy individual human needs. People have different needs, therefore different motivations. If employees can identify their predominant needs, they can seek situations in which motivation comes naturally. The five categories of work-related needs are:

♦ The need for achievement
The need for achievement may be defined as the need a person has for attention, high visibility and recognition by others.

If you are strong in this need, you enjoy being in the forefront of an activity. You should look for challenging work situations that offer opportunities for exposure.

♦ The need to affiliate
The need to affiliate is the need a person has to feel accepted as a member of the group with which one identifies.

Since the major goal of people with this need is to establish relationships, you are motivated by the informal interaction of work groups or teams.

♦ The need for appreciation
All human beings share a need to be reassured that we are appreciated for our contribution.

If this is your driving need, seek out organizations and bosses who believe in providing frequent recognition for accomplishments.

◆ **The need for control**
The need for control is often characterized by an ability to lead, persuade or influence others.

If your need in this area is high, you will be most motivated in jobs where you have authority, prestige and the opportunity to make things happen.

◆ **The need for financial security**
For many people, financial security and success is an ongoing need.

If this is a top need for you, you will generally respond most favorably to situations that involve making or saving money. Motivating situations include those in which cash incentives or stock options are used to reward performance.

Taking Charge of Your Career

In today's work environment, you can no longer depend on patriarchal organizations to chart your career path. The Organization Man was a corporate "lifer." But the average American beginning his or her career in the 1990s will probably work in ten or more jobs, for five or more employers, before retiring. This is according to *Workplace 2000: The Revolution Reshaping American Business* by Henry Conn and Joseph Boyett.

You are your own business, and no one else is responsible for your development. You cannot count on your employer to watch out for you, and you cannot rely on a mentor to bring you along. The progression and direction of your career is now up to you.

A training consultant at Hewlett-Packard puts it this way: "If there's a slowdown in the computer industry, an employee has to figure out what it means to him. That takes talking not only to people within the company, but to people at other companies, to stay on top of industry trends. *Those people who succeed are usually the first ones to recognize change and work with it.*"

Alternative Career Paths

For many people, upward mobility is the only acceptable and rewarding way to develop a career. Upward mobility provides additional status, responsibility, compensation and title. For those employees hoping to move up, simply slogging along and turning in a solid performance is no longer enough. You have to be perceived by others as someone who can step in and deliver immediately.

Although most employees equate *up* with success, there are four other viable career direction alternatives: moving across, moving down, staying put and moving out.

♦**Moving Across** - Horizontal, or lateral, moves involve changes in function and/or job title, usually without a corresponding change in salary or status. These are quickly becoming the choice of many change-adept professionals who use laterals to demonstrate their adaptive abilities and broadening skills. Moving laterally allows employees to learn about other areas of the organization, enlarge their professional network and develop various talents. In many companies, cross-training or job rotation programs are common ways to ensure that employees have sufficient background to be transferred in times of departmental cutbacks.

One of my clients, Patricia, has developed her entire career in lateral moves: Working for a local utility company, she started out laying gas lines and repairing them. Patricia then let her supervisors know she was interested in customer services, and took a lateral move into reading meters. After a couple of promotions, when she became a customer service supervisor, she discovered she was interested in organizational development. She moved laterally again into an organizational planning and development group. Soon after, she was promoted into management. Patricia now serves as an internal consultant on organizational issues.

♦**Moving Down** - Moving down is another option that our changing value system has made more feasible during the last few years. Many people are looking toward outside interests for self-fulfillment. They see the opportunity to move backward as a chance to free themselves from time- and energy-consuming positions.

A poll of seven hundred residents in Northern California found that a whopping 90 percent would like to see a two-track career system—a *fast track* and a slower track—offered by their companies. A study by Robert Half International found that the slower track was preferred by 82 percent of females polled, and 74 percent of males. Over half of the men in this study said they would give up 25 percent of their salaries for more personal or family time. Many of these respondents would view moving down as a real opportunity.

♦**Staying Put** - Sometimes the best opportunities are right where you are. In fact, when employees recognize the advantages open to them in their present assignments, it is not unusual for them to decide to remain in their current jobs a little longer.

For the employee who wants to stay put, but feels stagnated by a too-well-known job, this involves increasing the challenge of meaning of a current job, by looking for ways to use this work situation as a launching pad to future opportunities. This exercise has helped people to start thinking about ways to redesign work, to make it more rewarding:

1. Describe your ideal work situation.
2. Describe your current work situation.
3. How can you create more alignment between reality and your ideal?
4. What is one action you are willing to take to bring about this alignment?

♦**Moving Out** - Every employee wants to feel satisfied and challenged within the organization that employs him. Still, it is naive to assume that everyone's present employers will always meet these needs. Some individuals may choose to leave their present occupation, profession, industry or firm.

Charles Handy, author of *The Age of Unreason*, a book about the changing nature of work, states: "Instead of climbing up the ladder, people now have to develop a portfolio of skills and products that they can sell directly to a series of customers. We are all becoming people with portfolio careers."

Thousands of people are doing just that. They are assembling skills they can market in different industries. In the October 7, 1991, issue of *Business Week* magazine, it was stated that there is a dramatic change in the definition of work. "Jobs are increasingly determined by skills, and titles are meaningless. Companies want people who can solve problems and complete projects. Security derives from the salability of a 'can do' reputation in a job market that spans all industries."

A Personal Vision

When Alice was in Wonderland, she came to a place where the road she was following split into two forks. At this juncture, the Cheshire Cat appeared and Alice asked him which road she should take. The Cat said that it depended on where she was heading. "I don't really know," said Alice. "Then it really doesn't matter which way you go," answered the Cat.

Without an overall guiding purpose, the particular choices you make in your life and career *really do not matter.* A personal vision reflects your purpose in life. It gives you direction.

Having a personal sense of vision and purpose can be a matter of life and death. Many hard-working people know how to get things done in the workplace and feel a sense of direction only when given one by the organization. If your vision is set out for you at work, you can be sure it will disappear when you lose or leave the job. Much of the literature on retirement indicates that people without purpose in retirement are not known for breaking records for longevity. Seven in ten retirees die within two years. It appears that if these people had established some personal vision in life, that would have been a driving force which resulted in their living much longer.

Discovering your personal vision is the cornerstone for using your vitality and creativity. To begin the process of looking within for vision and purpose, look back in time, from childhood on, to those events when you felt most alive, joyful and fulfilled.

1. Draw a lifeline starting as far back as you can remember. Draw your lifeline as a graph with the peaks representing the highs in your life and the valleys representing the lows.

2. Next to each peak, write a word or two that identifies the peak experience. Do the same for the valleys.

3. Now go over each peak and elaborate on why this was a peak experience for you. Do the same for the valleys.

4. Analyze your notes. What themes and patterns are revealed by the peaks and valleys in your life? What personal strengths and preferences are revealed? What do these themes and patterns tell you about your personal vision of success? How can this insight be helpful in facing the future?

5. Write a short vision statement—try for 25 words or less. Find a picture or symbol that represents your vision. Keep your written statement and picture/symbol as concrete reminders of your vision.

6. Like anything else in life, in the future your personal vision may evolve and transform. At least once a year, do a *reality check* to see if your stated purpose still holds true for you.

Here is Ralph Waldo Emerson's personal vision statement, as reflected in his definition of success:

WHAT IS SUCCESS?

To laugh often and much;

To win the respect of intelligent persons and the affection of children;

To earn the approval of honest critics and endure the betrayal of false friends;

To appreciate beauty;

To find the best in others;

To give of one's self without the slightest thought of return;

To have accomplished a task, whether by a healthy child, a rescued soul, a garden patch or a redeemed social condition;

To have played and laughed with enthusiasm and sung with exaltation;

To know that even one life has breathed easier because you have lived;

This is to have succeeded.

Choosing to Change

If you put a frog in a pot of cold water and heat the water slowly, the frog will eventually get boiled. The hapless frog simply becomes too comfortable to know when its behavior should have changed.

Of course, we are not frogs. We are human beings with an enormous capacity for change. People can be motivated to change by *either positive or negative motivators. Positive motivation* accompanies changes that originate out *of our personal vision*—those changes we choose because we are internally compelled to do so. This kind of positive motivation can be very powerful, because it forces us to develop more of our potential. And when that process is underway, it leads to an ongoing progression of changes and growth.

But sometimes it takes a negative experience to precipitate a life- or career-altering change. Many years ago, a young man mustered enough courage to ask a young woman to dance. After several minutes on the dance floor, the woman bluntly told the man that he was a lousy dancer. She complained that he "danced like a truck driver." Crushed, the young man determined never to be that embarrassed again, so he began taking dance lessons. Over time, he developed a passion for dancing and continued to dance for many years. At the time of his death in March 1991, Arthur Murray's name was almost synonymous with the word *dance*. Over 500 dance schools were named after him, and he had taught dancing on his national television program for eleven straight years.

The Process of Positive Transitions

As I mentioned in Chapter 7 of this book, even the most positive change is accompanied by an emotional transition process. Every change begins with an ending—something that you must give up or leave behind. This is true for all kinds of change. But when change is positively anticipated or *chosen,* emotional reactions are different from the emotions inherent in transitions of negative or *imposed* change. While many people have come to expect— and think of as *natural*—the emotional reaction to negative change, few are prepared for the unique stages of positive transition.

Researchers studying individuals from various organizations, including the Peace Corps, delineated these stages of positive transition: Elation, disenchantment, detachment and acceptance.

◆**Elation -** Positive transition begins with the emotional stage of elation. You have just been notified that you won the corporate-wide suggestion contest, you have been given an awaited raise, or you have been promoted to the job of your dreams. You may be surprised, you may even be slightly fearful, but you are surely elated at the good news.

◆**Disenchantment -** Sure, you were elated at first, but you were elated by the fantasy of what you *thought* the change would be. When reality hits, you find that your co-workers are jealous of the prize you won, the taxes out of your raise leave you with little more than you had before, or the new promotion means that you will have to stay longer at work and have less time with your family. Whatever else it may be—the positive experience is not exactly what you *imagined* it would be. And so, naturally enough, you experience a period of disenchantment.

♦**Detachment** - If you stay disenchanted, you will probably revert to your old situation. Before one of my private clients successfully lost 35 pounds, she fantasized that her life would be *perfect* when she was a size eight. Instead, she found that her best friend no longer spoke to her, and her husband was jealously possessive of her time. Slowly but surely, she regained the weight.

But most of the time you do not remain disenchanted. Instead, you successfully come to terms with the reality of the situation and detach from the fantasy.

♦**Acceptance** - The final emotional stage is acceptance. So the reality of the situation is not the perfect solution you imagined it might be. Now you take a close look at the genuine opportunities within the change, and decide if this is still a good deal for you. If it is, you consciously choose to commit to the change—imperfect and wonderful as it actually is.

Preparing to Change

Change is never easy. Even those changes we elect to make—changes which we have chosen because they are in our best interest—require preparation and strategy to accomplish. After working with thousands of individuals going through personal and professional transitions, I have developed a set of strategic questions for those choosing to make a change. When a person can answer all the questions, he or she is prepared for successful change. Here are the questions:

What specific behaviors do you want/need to change?
Why do you want to make the change?
What is your strategy for change?
What obstacles must you prepare for?
What resources will you need?
How are you planning to deal with failure?
How will you reward your success?

If we take these questions one at a time, I can explain how they apply to a variety of changes. Start with the first question: *What specific behaviors do you want to change?*

There are many ways to reach a goal. Suppose you want to reduce your weight. It is not enough to set a particular weight goal. You must decide exactly how you want to reach that objective. How do you choose to change your behavior to lose weight? For instance, the specific behavioral changes in a weight-loss program could be any—or a combination—of the following:

- ♦ Go on a specific diet for a specific length of time.
- ♦ Reduce daily calories by using a calorie-counter.
- ♦ Eat half as much as you have in the past.
- ♦ Increase your exercise program.
- ♦ Eliminate certain high-calorie, high-cholesterol foods from your diet.
- ♦ Develop new nutrition and eating habits for life.
- ♦ Enroll in a liquid diet program run by your local clinic or hospital.
- ♦ Stop all snacking between meals.
- ♦ Eat several, very small meals every day.
- ♦ Fast for one day each week.

While any of these behavioral changes could help you reach your objective, they each take a different strategic set of actions to succeed. For example, if you decide to enroll in a liquid diet program, you will face unique social situations. How will you handle invitations to dinner when you cannot eat food? Will you decline the invitations, bring your liquid diet with you, or what? If you decide to increase your physical exercise, exactly where and when do you plan to do so? What kind of exercise will you do?

After you have decided on the exact behavioral changes required, the next question becomes most important: *Why do you want to make the change?* bored, no chare y soretry else

In my private practice, I became well known for my success in aiding smokers to become nonsmokers in a single counseling session. The *secret* of my success was the way I chose which clients I would work with. When a potential client telephoned and said that her doctor wanted her to quit smoking, I'd reply, "Good. I'll make an appointment for your doctor. And when there's anything that **you** want to do, be sure and call me back."

Helping a client change behavior from smoker to nonsmoker is no easy matter. I learned early in my career that the only motivation strong enough to support an individual through this challenging experience was *personal motivation*. No one quits smoking because her doctor—or her spouse or her children—wants her to. To ensure a client's success, it was important that the motivation for the change came from within. Once I was assured of a person's personal desire to be a nonsmoker, I could base my entire approach around strengthening and focusing that most powerful source of motivation.

Do not skim over this question. Think deeply about all the reasons why you want to make a change. List your reasons. Look at the list often, to strengthen your resolve. Remember that no worthwhile endeavor comes easily. Change is awkward and uncomfortable—especially at first. The best way to overcome the discomfort is to become so focused on your desire to change that it becomes a burning passion that will not be denied.

What is your strategy for change? Outlining a strategy for the stages of change begins by visualizing the completed goal and then planning backward to identify the steps necessary to reach that objective.

One of my clients wanted to change vocations and to pursue a career as a fiction writer. He set his goal, and then worked backward through the necessary steps: 1) Go to night school and brush up on writing skills; 2) get up early and start writing a little every day; 3) increase savings for a monetary "cushion"; 4) sign up for an early retirement next time it is offered by his employer; 5) sell his large house and move to smaller, less expensive accommodations; 6) join a professional authors' association.

When you have outlined the steps of change, it is time to list all the possible obstacles—including yourself—that could get in the way of your successful change. *What obstacles must you prepare for?*

- When I wanted to begin an exercise program, my busy schedule was my greatest obstacle.
- A student wanted to get an "A" on his history paper. He feared that his procrastination would get in the way.
- A client who wanted to accept a relocation offer thought that her husband's reluctance to leave the area was the biggest obstacle to her acceptance.
- An employee who had a great idea for a work-related change felt that his boss would take all the credit.

Of course it is not enough simply to list all obstacles. The next step is to strategize ways to overcome those obstacles with resources. *What resources will you need?*

- To guarantee that I would clear time for exercise classes, I wrote them in my appointment book; I learned to treat these *appointments* as important scheduled events.
- The student enlisted the aid of a friend who also had to write an important paper. They accompanied each other on scheduled trips to the library, and made an agreement that either student who missed a library session had to type the paper of the other.
- My client relied on a series of resources to help convince her husband to make the move: She brought brochures of the area. She researched the nearby golf courses—her husband's favorite sport—and arranged for her husband to accompany her on a field trip to the new location. She agreed to rent—not sell—their old home for one year, and to use that year as a trial period.
- The employee with the great idea decided to build a coalition of *backers* for the idea before presenting it to his boss. In this way, he figured, his proposal would have more support and—at the same time—co-workers would witness that the idea was originally his.

The next question often shocks people. *How are you planning to deal with failure?* I figure it is a legitimate question. I know for sure that your successes will not stop you, so if your failures cannot—then nothing will. Planning for failure is one way of strengthening your resolve to persevere through thick and thin.

When Winston Churchill was asked to address a graduating class, his best advice for success was contained in these words: "Never give up. Never, never, never, never, never, never, never, never . . ."

If you are on a diet, how are you going to deal with the day when you go off your diet and over-eat? Are you going to use that isolated event as an excuse to give up the diet? If you are looking for a job, how are you going to deal with one rejection after another? Will you allow your disappointment to put an end to your job search? If you are trying to learn to operate the new computer program and you just cannot seem to understand it, how will you deal with those feelings of incompetence? Are you going let them stop you from trying again?

To encourage persistence, you need a plan for dealing with failure. Specifically, what are you going to do? Are you going to learn from failure, release it and move on? Are you going to reconnect with your internal motivation? Are you going to develop a plan for dealing with similar situations if they occur in the future? Are you going to remind yourself that every great person failed at something—that failure is an integral part of change? Are you going to make fun of—or make friends with—failure?

If you allow for the possibility of failures—or setbacks or disappointments—and develop a strategy for dealing with them, you prepare yourself to—no matter what—*never* give up.

To make a personal, permanent change takes time. You must rehearse the new behavior, while seeking feedback and adjustment. You must practice and visualize the accomplished goal repeatedly. You must plan for obstacles and setbacks while developing the necessary resources. And you must stay motivated and committed to the change. This is hard work.

Therefore, it startles me to see how many people plan extensive personal change, requiring tremendous determination and effort, and never consider the last of my questions: *How will you reward your success?*

Several years ago, the American Management Association (AMA) conducted a survey, with 6,000 participants across the United States. The survey had only two questions: 1) Do you get enough recognition at work? 2) Would you do a better job if you got more recognition?

The response was overwhelming. Ninety-seven percent of the respondents said *no*—they did not get enough recognition at work. Ninety-eight percent replied *yes*—they would do a better job if they received more recognition.

To the AMA, it pointed out inadequate management practices. Obviously, not enough managers were doing a good enough job at recognizing and rewarding the people who report to them.

To me, however, the results of the study brought another disturbing aspect of the situation to light: Most of us were waiting—unrealistically it seems—for someone else to say "good work!"

Change-adept employees take control by finding ways to "catch themselves doing things right." They acknowledge their own accomplishments. The process of rewarding a successful change is part of their ongoing personal recognition program.

Are you taking full advantage of opportunities to celebrate successful change? Every time you reward an accomplished change by toasting yourself with a glass of champagne, or taking yourself out to dinner, or buying a bouquet of flowers for your desk, or patting yourself on the back, you are reinforcing your self-image as a change-adept individual and increasing your ability to make additional changes, now and in the future.

A CHECKLIST

- ☐ Do I have a proactive response to change?
- ☐ Am I values-driven?
- ☐ Do I know what motivates me?
- ☐ Am I aware that the full responsibility for my career rests with me?
- ☐ Have I taken stock of where I now stand in my life, to see if the goals and dreams of my past still reflect my current values and needs?
- ☐ Am I led by my personal vision?
- ☐ Am I prepared for the emotional transition process of positive change?
- ☐ Do I have a detailed "project plan" for changes I desire to make?

Conclusion

As the speed and scope of change increasingly requires corporations to reinvent themselves, the ability of individuals to respond effectively becomes a major criterion for success. I would like to close this book with a few final observations:

♦ Leaders of this era are those individuals at all levels of an organization who are change-adept—willing and able to capitalize on change opportunities, for themselves and their companies.

♦ Even with the trauma and turmoil of constant change, or perhaps because of it, there has never been a better time than right now for individuals who want to make a difference, and want to contribute substantially to the workplace.

♦ No matter how overwhelming the winds of change may feel—and believe me, they feel overwhelming, at some time, to all of us—they really cannot compare to the power and resilience of the human spirit.

About the Author

Carol Kinsey Goman, Ph.D., president of Kinsey Consulting Services, is an internationally recognized expert on the "human side" of organizational change. She has served as adjunct faculty for John F. Kennedy University, in their international MBA program, and for the Executive Education Department at the University of California in Berkeley. She is an instructor for the United States Chamber of Commerce at their Institutes for Leadership Development. Her published books include *Change-Busting: 50 Ways to Sabotage Organizational Change, Creativity in Business, Managing for Commitment,* and *The Loyalty Factor: Building Trust in Today's Workplace.*

Addressing conferences and conventions around the world, Carol's upbeat style has earned her a deserved reputation as one of America's best keynote speakers. Her programs are delivered to corporations and professional associations for clients that include: A.T.&T., Motorola, Bank of America, DuPont, Harsco Corporation, Kaiser Permanente, the American Chamber of Commerce in Hong Kong, National Provident in New Zealand, KF Group in Sweden, Bell Canada, and the Puerto Rico Hotel and Tourism Association.

For more information on her books and programs, please contact:

Carol Kinsey Goman, Ph.D.
Kinsey Consulting Services
P.O. Box 8255
Berkeley, CA 94707
(510) 943-7850 - fax (510) 524-9577